VERY SHORT INTRODUCTIONS are for anyone wanting a stimulating and accessible way into a new subject. They are written by experts, and have been translated into more than 40 different languages.

The series began in 1995, and now covers a wide variety of topics in every discipline. The VSI library now contains over 400 volumes—a Very Short Introduction to everything from Psychology and Philosophy of Science to American History and Relativity—and continues to grow in every subject area.

Very Short Introductions available now:

ACCOUNTING Christopher Nobes
ADVERTISING Winston Fletcher
AFRICAN AMERICAN RELIGION
    Eddie S. Glaude Jr.
AFRICAN HISTORY John Parker and
    Richard Rathbone
AFRICAN RELIGIONS Jacob K. Olupona
AGNOSTICISM Robin Le Poidevin
ALEXANDER THE GREAT
    Hugh Bowden
AMERICAN HISTORY Paul S. Boyer
AMERICAN IMMIGRATION
    David A. Gerber
AMERICAN LEGAL HISTORY
    G. Edward White
AMERICAN POLITICAL HISTORY
    Donald Critchlow
AMERICAN POLITICAL PARTIES
    AND ELECTIONS L. Sandy Maisel
AMERICAN POLITICS Richard M. Valelly
THE AMERICAN PRESIDENCY
    Charles O. Jones
THE AMERICAN REVOLUTION
    Robert J. Allison
AMERICAN SLAVERY
    Heather Andrea Williams
THE AMERICAN WEST Stephen Aron
AMERICAN WOMEN'S HISTORY
    Susan Ware
ANAESTHESIA Aidan O'Donnell
ANARCHISM Colin Ward
ANCIENT ASSYRIA Karen Radner
ANCIENT EGYPT Ian Shaw
ANCIENT EGYPTIAN ART AND
    ARCHITECTURE Christina Riggs

ANCIENT GREECE Paul Cartledge
THE ANCIENT NEAR EAST
    Amanda H. Podany
ANCIENT PHILOSOPHY Julia Annas
ANCIENT WARFARE Harry Sidebottom
ANGELS David Albert Jones
ANGLICANISM Mark Chapman
THE ANGLO-SAXON AGE John Blair
THE ANIMAL KINGDOM
    Peter Holland
ANIMAL RIGHTS David DeGrazia
THE ANTARCTIC Klaus Dodds
ANTISEMITISM Steven Beller
ANXIETY Daniel Freeman and
    Jason Freeman
THE APOCRYPHAL GOSPELS
    Paul Foster
ARCHAEOLOGY Paul Bahn
ARCHITECTURE Andrew Ballantyne
ARISTOCRACY William Doyle
ARISTOTLE Jonathan Barnes
ART HISTORY Dana Arnold
ART THEORY Cynthia Freeland
ASTROBIOLOGY David C. Catling
ATHEISM Julian Baggini
AUGUSTINE Henry Chadwick
AUSTRALIA Kenneth Morgan
AUTISM Uta Frith
THE AVANT GARDE David Cottington
THE AZTECS David Carrasco
BACTERIA Sebastian G. B. Amyes
BARTHES Jonathan Culler
THE BEATS David Sterritt
BEAUTY Roger Scruton
BESTSELLERS John Sutherland

Law: A Very Short Introduction

Available soon:

For more information visit our website
www.oup.com/vsi/

Raymond Wacks

LAW

A Very Short Introduction
SECOND EDITION

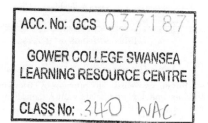

OXFORD
UNIVERSITY PRESS

OXFORD
UNIVERSITY PRESS

Great Clarendon Street, Oxford, OX2 6DP,
United Kingdom

Oxford University Press is a department of the University of Oxford.
It furthers the University's objective of excellence in research, scholarship,
and education by publishing worldwide. Oxford is a registered trade mark of
Oxford University Press in the UK and in certain other countries

First edition published 2008
Second edition published 2015

Impression: 5

Published in the United States of America by Oxford University Press
198 Madison Avenue, New York, NY 10016, United States of America

British Library Cataloguing in Publication Data

Data available

Library of Congress Control Number: 2015938931

ISBN 978-0-19-874562-4

Printed in Great Britain by
Ashford Colour Press Ltd, Gosport, Hampshire

Contents

Preface

Rarely do the words 'law' and 'brevity' inhabit the same sentence. The notorious verbosity of the law may suggest that any attempt to condense even its rudiments is an undertaking of utopian, if not quixotic, proportions. But this is the improbable task I have undertaken in these pages. I have attempted to distil the essentials of the complex phenomenon of law: its roots, branches, purpose, practice, institutions, and future. My purpose is to introduce the lay reader—including the prospective or novice student of law, politics, and other social sciences—to the fundamentals of law and legal systems, avoiding as much technical jargon as possible.

I hope too that this little volume will encourage curiosity about the intriguing nature of law, and stimulate further reflection upon, and exploration into, the central role it plays in all of our lives. Those in search of a deeper understanding of the numerous facets of the law will want to turn to some of the many works that I list in the Further reading section. There is also, of course, a wealth of admirable online legal resources, some of which are provided in Chapter 6 and in the Legal sources section.

It is important to stress that though the emphasis of the book is on the Western secular legal tradition (the common law and the civil law), I include brief accounts of other legal systems, such as Islamic law, customary law, and certain mixed systems, in order to offer an introduction to 'law' in its most general sense. I do, however, confess my predisposition toward the common law. This prejudice, if that is what it is, might be defended by pointing to what I see as a perceptible shift towards the globalization of various features of the common law. But the explanation is less arcane. English is the language in which the book is written by one who has spent most of his working life in common law jurisdictions. My limited proficiency in foreign languages dictates that all the sources—including those related to non-common law systems—are in English. Despite this encumbrance, I have attempted to curtail any gratuitous assumptions about the law that may spring from my own experience which, as it happens, is unusually varied. I studied and taught law in a mixed legal system (South Africa) as well as in two common law jurisdictions (England and Hong Kong), and I now live in a civil law country (Italy). My nomadic existence could, I suppose, be tendered as evidence in mitigation of any prejudice I may be guilty of exhibiting in these pages.

Serendipitously, two of these jurisdictions are particularly instructive; both underwent seismic transformations during the 1990s, entailing fundamental legal change. In 1992 the legal edifice of apartheid was demolished; two years later Nelson Mandela was elected President of the 'new' South Africa with its democratic constitution, bill of rights, and constitutional court. And in 1997, Hong Kong's metamorphosis from British colony to Chinese Special Administrative Region was, fundamentally, a matter of law. The form and structure of this improbable creature—a capitalist enclave within a nominally socialist state—is guaranteed by Hong Kong's Basic Law that safeguards the maintenance of the existing common law.

If there is a lesson to be learnt from these two constitutional episodes, it is the perhaps rather prosaic truth that the law is an imperfect yet crucial vehicle by which both to conserve and transform society. It would be rash to undervalue the capacity of an effective legal system and the rule of law to ensure the indispensable virtues of liberty, equality, certainty, generality, safety, and predictability. Few societies attain genuine harmony and accord; yet in the absence of a sound legal system the descent into chaos and conflict would surely beleaguer our increasingly polarized planet. The rising threat of Islamic terror poses formidable challenges to the ability of the law to strike a balance between freedom and security.

To abridge—without oversimplifying—the central characteristics of the law entailed countless cold-blooded judgments. Numerous chunks of text were reluctantly dispatched to my swelling recycle bin. I can only hope that in charting the central terrain of contemporary law, the frontiers I have drawn are neither excessively narrow nor unreasonably wide. I have endeavoured to plot the most prominent features of the topography of the ever-shifting landscape of the law, acknowledging, of course, that much lies on its periphery.

It is also important to emphasize that the law cannot properly be understood without an awareness of its social, political, moral, and economic dimensions. Legal theory or jurisprudence seeks to uncover many of these deeper philosophical elements that explain the complex phenomenon of law and the legal process. Chapter 3 seeks to elucidate the controversial tension between the law and the moral practices adopted by society. I have resisted further excursions into the often impenetrable thicket of legal philosophy, both because it lies beyond the modest objectives of this work, and in the hope that readers in pursuit of an introduction to this stimulating discipline may wish to turn to my *Philosophy of Law: A Very Short Introduction*, 2nd edition (Oxford University Press, 2014) which may—optimistically—be regarded as a companion volume to this one.

This new edition has been considerably improved as a result of the helpful and constructive comments and suggestions generously tendered by the anonymous readers of the manuscript. I am greatly indebted to them.

Gratitude is also owed to my cheerful co-conspirators of Great Clarendon Street. Special thanks to Andrea Keegan, Jenny Nugee, Deborah Protheroe, and Dan Harding.

Without the enduring love, encouragement, and support of my wife, Penelope (felicitously, a barrister), little would be possible. Over this loyal subject, her sovereignty is unbounded; her word law.

Law

List of illustrations

Chapter 1
Law's roots

Board a bus. The law is there. You have almost certainly entered into a contract to pay the fare to your destination. Alight before you have paid, and the long arm of the criminal law may be expected to pursue you. The bus is involved in an accident. The law is ready to determine who is responsible for the injury you sustained.

Your job, your home, your relationships, your very life—and your death—all, and more, are managed, controlled, and directed by the law. It lies at the heart of every society, protecting rights, imposing duties, and establishing a framework for the conduct of almost all social, political, and economic activity. Punishing offenders, compensating the injured, and enforcing agreements are merely some of the tasks of a modern legal system. In addition, it strives to achieve justice, promote freedom, uphold the rule of law, and protect security.

To the layman, however, the law often seems a highly technical, bewildering mystery, with its antiquated and sometimes impenetrable jargon, obsolete procedures, and interminable stream of Byzantine statutes, subordinate legislation, and judgments of the courts. Moreover, lawyers frequently appear to be looking backwards. The doctrine of precedent, hallmark of the common law, dictates that what has gone before is what now should be, thereby affording a measure of certainty and predictability in a precarious world.

But the law does not stand still. Globalization, rapid advances in technology, and the growth of administrative regulation all place increasing strain on the law. Domestic legal systems are expected to respond to, and even anticipate, these changes, while many look to international law to settle disputes between states, punish malevolent dictators, and create a better world. These are among the numerous challenges to which contemporary legal systems are meant to rise.

The law is rarely uncontroversial. While lawyers and politicians habitually venerate its merits, reformers bewail its inadequacies, and sceptics refute the law's often self-righteous espousal of justice, liberty, and the rule of law. Few, however, would deny that, in most societies, law has become a significant instrument for progress and the improvement of our social, political, moral, and economic life. Think of the transformation that legal rules have wrought in respect of numerous aspects of our lives that were once considered personal: the promotion of sexual and racial equality, safety at work and play, healthier food, candour in commerce, and a host of other worthy aspirations. Laws to protect human rights, the environment, and our personal security have mushroomed. Nothing seems beyond the reach of the law. This boom in the law-making business renders it impractical both for citizens to become acquainted with its myriad rules, and for the authorities to enforce them.

The law is always news. Murders, mergers, marriages, misfortunes, and mendacity are daily media fodder, especially when the misbehaviour is played out in court. Sensationalist trials concerning celebrities are only the small tip of a large iceberg. Lawsuits are a negligible part of the law, as will become evident in the following chapters.

But what *is* law? In very broad terms, two principal answers have been given to this deceptively simple question. On the one hand is the belief that law consists of a set of universal moral principles in accordance with nature. This view (adopted by so-called natural lawyers) has a long history dating back to ancient Greece. For so-called legal positivists, on the other hand, law is little more than a collection of valid rules, commands, or norms that may lack any moral content. Others perceive the law as fundamentally a vehicle for the protection of individual rights, the attainment of justice, or economic, political, and sexual equality. Few consider that the law can be divorced from its social context. The social, political, moral, and economic dimensions of the law are essential to a proper understanding of its workaday operation. This is especially true in times of change. It is important to recognize the fragility of formalism; we skate on dangerously thin ice when we neglect the contingent nature of the law and its values. Reflection upon the nature of law may sometimes seem disconcertingly abstruse. More than occasionally, however, it reveals important insights into who we are and what we do. The nature and consequences of these different positions should become apparent before long.

The genesis of law

Despite the importance of law in society, its manifestation in the form of general codes first appears only around 3000 BC. Prior to the advent of writing, laws exist only in the form of custom. And the absence of written law retards the capacity of these rules to provide lasting or extensive application.

Among the first written codes is that of Hammurabi, king and creator of the Babylonian empire. It appeared in about 1760 BC, and is one of the earliest instances of a ruler proclaiming a systematic corpus of law to his people so that they are able to know their rights and duties. Engraved on a black stone slab (that may be seen in the Louvre in Paris), the code contains some 300 sections with rules relating to a broad array of activities ranging from the punishment that is to be inflicted on a false witness (death) to that to be meted out to a builder whose house collapses killing the owner (death). The code is almost entirely devoid of defences or excuses, a very early example of strict liability!

The king was, in fact, acknowledging the existence of even earlier laws (of which we have only the barest of evidence), which his code implies. In truth, therefore, the code echoes customs that preceded the reign of this ancient monarch (see Figure 1).

A more striking example of early law making may be found in the laws of the Athenian statesman Solon in the 6th century BC. Regarded by the ancient Greeks as one of the Seven Wise Men, he was granted the authority to legislate to assist Athens in overcoming its social and economic crisis. His laws were extensive, including significant reforms to the economy, politics, marriage, and crime and punishment. He divided Athenian society into five classes based on financial standing. One's obligations (including tax liability) depended on one's class. He cancelled debts for which the peasants had pledged their land or their bodies, thereby terminating the institution of serfdom.

To resolve disputes between higher- and lower-ranked citizens, the Romans, in about 450 BC, issued, in tablet form, a compilation of laws known as the Twelve Tables. A commission of ten men (*Decemviri*) was appointed in about 455 BC to draft a code of law binding on all Romans—the privileged class (the patricians) and the common people (the plebeians)—which the magistrates (two consuls) were required to enforce. The result was a compilation of numerous statutes, most derived from prevailing custom, which filled ten bronze tablets. The plebeians were unimpressed with the result, and a second commission of ten was appointed in 450 BC. It added another two tablets.

1. The Code of Hammurabi created by the King of Babylon in about 1760 BC. It is a well-preserved diorite stele setting out 282 laws that provide a fascinating insight into life under his rule.

During the period of the so-called classical jurists, between the 1st century BC and the middle of the 3rd century AD, Roman law achieved a condition of considerable sophistication. Indeed, so prolific were these jurists (Gauis, Ulpian, Papinian, Paul, and several others) that their enormous output became hopelessly unwieldy. Between AD 529 and 534, therefore, the Eastern emperor, Justinian, ordered that these manifold texts be reduced to a systematic, comprehensive codification. The three resulting books, the *Corpus Juris Civilis* (comprising the Digest, Codex, and Institutes), were to be treated as definitive: a conclusive statement of the law that required no interpretation. But this illusion of unconditional certainty soon became evident: the codification was both excessively lengthy (close to a million words) and too detailed to admit of easy application (see Figure 2).

Its meticulous detail proved, however, to be its strength. More than 600 years after the fall of the Western Roman Empire, Europe witnessed a revival in the study of Roman law. And Justinian's codification, which had remained in force in parts of Western Europe, was the perfect specimen upon which European lawyers could conduct their experiments. With the establishment in about AD 1088 in Bologna of the first university in Western Europe, and the burgeoning of universities throughout Europe in the succeeding four centuries, students of law were taught Justinian's law alongside canon law. Moreover, the contradictions and complexity of the codes turned out to be an advantage, since, despite the emperor's fantasy of finality, the rules were susceptible to interpretation and adaptation to suit the requirements of the time. In this way, Roman civil law spread throughout most of Europe—in the face of its detractors during the Renaissance and the Reformation.

By the 18th century, however, it was recognized that more concise codes were called for. Justinian's codification was replaced by several codes that sought brevity, accessibility, and comprehensiveness. The Napoleonic code of 1804 came close to

2. The Byzantine Roman Emperor Justinian, depicted here in one of the striking mosaics in Ravenna, oversaw the revision and codification of Roman law into the *Corpus Juris Civilis*, consisting of the Digest (or Pandects), Institutes, Codex, and Novellae.

fulfilling these lofty aspirations. It was exported by colonization to large tracts of Western and Southern Europe and thence to Latin America, and it exerted an enormous influence throughout Europe. A more technical, abstract code was enacted in Germany in 1900. What it lacks in user-friendliness, it makes up for in its astonishing comprehensiveness. Known as the BGB, its influence has also been considerable: it afforded a model for the civil codes of China, Japan, Taiwan, Greece, and the Baltic states.

The Western legal tradition

The Western legal tradition has a number of distinctive features, in particular:

- A fairly clear demarcation between legal institutions (including adjudication, legislation, and the rules they spawn), on the one hand, and other types of institutions, on the other; legal authority in the former exerting supremacy over political institutions.

- The nature of legal doctrine which comprises the principal source of the law and the basis of legal training, knowledge, and institutional practice.

- The concept of law as a coherent, organic body of rules and principles with its own internal logic.

- The existence and specialized training of lawyers and other legal personnel.

While some of these characteristics may occur in other legal traditions, they differ in respect of both the importance they accord to, and their attitude towards, the precise role of law in society. Law, especially the rule of law, is in Western Europe a fundamental element in the formation and significance of society itself. This veneration of law and the legal process also shapes the exercise of government, domestically and internationally, by contemporary Western democracies.

The ideal of the rule of law, though its roots may be found in Magna Carta of 1215 (which rejected the idea of unchecked, unaccountable royal power), is most closely associated with the English constitutional scholar Albert Venn Dicey, who in his celebrated work *An Introduction to the Study of the Law of the Constitution*, published in 1885, expounded the fundamental precepts of the (unwritten) British constitution, and especially the concept of the rule of law which, in his view, consisted of the following three principles:

- The absolute supremacy or predominance of regular law as opposed to the influence of arbitrary power.
- Equality before the law or the equal subjection of all classes to the ordinary law of the land administered by the ordinary courts.
- The law of the constitution is a consequence of the rights of individuals as defined and enforced by the courts.

Contemporary views of the rule of law seek to adapt Dicey's rather formal conception to substantive matters of legality, authority, and other elements of democratic governance. For example, one writer adds flesh to the bare bones of Dicey's principles by arguing that the rule of law performs a vital role in enabling individuals to plan their lives. To do so, he suggests, the law ought to be prospective (as opposed to retrospective); relatively stable; that particular laws should be directed by open, general, and clear rules; that the courts should be independent and accessible; and that those who enforce the law should not have unrestricted discretion. But compliance with these values does not guarantee a just society. It is possible for a wicked legal system to satisfy these norms, as occurred to a large extent, for example, in South Africa under apartheid.

Civil law and common law

The system of codified law that obtains in most of Europe, South America, and elsewhere (see Figure 3) is known as civil law, in

3. Although civil law systems predominate, the common law and, to a lesser extent, religious and customary law, apply in several countries.

contrast to the common law system that applies in England and Wales, former British colonies, the United States, and most of Canada. Civil law is frequently divided into four groups. First, is French civil law, which also exists in Belgium and Luxembourg, the Canadian province of Quebec, Italy, Spain, and their former colonies, including those in Africa and South America. Second, German civil law, which is, in large part, applied in Austria, Switzerland, Portugal, Greece, Turkey, Japan, South Korea, and Taiwan. Third, Scandinavian civil law exists in Sweden, Denmark, Norway, and Iceland. Finally, Chinese (or China) law combines elements of civil law and socialist law. This is by no means an airtight classification. For example, Italian, Portuguese, and Brazilian law have, over the last century, moved closer to German law as their civil codes increasingly adopted key elements of the German civil code. The Russian civil code is partly a translation of the Dutch code.

Though the two traditions—common law and civil law—have, over the last century, grown closer, there are at least five significant differences between the two systems. First, the common law is essentially unwritten, non-textual law that was fashioned by medieval lawyers and the judges of the royal courts before whom they submitted their arguments. Indeed, it may be that this entrenched oral tradition, supported by a strong monarchy, developed by experts before the revival in the study of Roman law, explains why that system was never 'received' in England.

Codification has been resisted by generations of common lawyers, though this hostility has been weaker in the United States, where, since its establishment in 1923, the American Law Institute (a group of lawyers, judges, and legal scholars) has published a number of 'restatements of the law' (including those on contract, property, agency, torts, and trusts) to 'address uncertainty in the law through a restatement of basic legal subjects that would tell judges and lawyers what the law was'. They seek to clarify rather than codify the law. Their standing as secondary authority is demonstrated by their widespread (though not always consistent) acceptance by American courts. More significant is the Uniform Commercial Code (UCC), which establishes rules in respect of a number of key commercial transactions that apply across the country. With fifty states with different laws, uniformity in respect of commercial transactions is obviously vital. Imagine the confusion in the absence of such standardization: you live in New York and buy a car in New Jersey that is made in Michigan, warehoused in Maine, and delivered to your home.

Second, the common law is casuistic: the building blocks are cases rather than, as in the civil law system, texts. Ask any American, Australian, or Antiguan law student how most of his or her study time is spent. The answer will almost certainly be 'reading cases'. Question their counterparts from Argentina, Austria, or Algeria, and they will allude to the civil and penal codes they persistently peruse. The consequence of the common lawyer's preoccupation with what the judges say—rather than what the codes declare—is a more pragmatic, less theoretical approach to legal problem solving.

Third, in view of the centrality of court decisions, the common law elevates the doctrine of precedent to a supreme position in the legal system. This doctrine means both that previous decisions of courts that involve substantially similar facts ought to govern present cases, and that the judgments of higher courts are binding on those lower in the judicial hierarchy. The justification for the idea is that it engenders constancy, predictability, and objectivity, while allowing for judges to 'distinguish' apparently binding precedents on the ground that the case before them differs from them in some material respect.

A fourth generalization is that while the common law proceeds from the premise 'where there is a remedy, there is a right', the civil law tradition generally adopts the opposite position: 'where there is a right, there is a remedy'. If the common law is essentially remedial, rather than rights-based, in its outlook, this is plainly a result of the so-called writ system under which, from the 12th century in England, litigation could not commence without a writ issued on the authority of the king. Every claim had its own formal writ. So, for example, the writ of debt was a prerequisite to any action to recover money owing, and the writ of right existed to recover land. In the 17th century, the ancient writ of *habeas corpus* (literally 'you must produce the body') was a vital check on arbitrary power, for it required the production of a person detained without trial to be brought before a court. In the absence of a legal justification for his imprisonment, the judge could order the individual to be liberated. It took a century for civil law jurisdictions to accept this fundamental attribute of a free society.

Finally, in the 13th century, the common law introduced trial by jury for both criminal and civil cases. The jury decides on the facts of the case; the judge determines the law. Trial by jury has remained a fundamental feature of the common law. This separation between facts and law was never adopted by civil law systems. It also illustrates the importance of the oral tradition of common law as against the essential role of written argument employed by the civil law (see Box 1).

Box 1 The common law, chaos, and codification

[L]ife might be much simpler if the common law consisted of a code of rules, identifiable by reference to source rules, but the reality of the matter is that it is all much more chaotic than that, and the only way to make the common law conform to the ideal would be to codify the system, which would then cease to be common law at all. The myth, for that is what it is, owes its attractiveness to another ideal, that of the rule of law, not men.... It consequently distorts the nature of the system to conceive of the common law as a set of rules, an essentially precise notion, as if one could in principle both state the rules of the common law and count them like so many sheep, or engrave them on tablets of stone.

A. W. B. Simpson, 'The Common Law and Legal Theory'

There are also certain jurisdictions, such as Scotland, that, though their legal systems are not codified, preserve varying degrees of Roman influence. On the other hand, some jurisdictions have avoided the impact of Roman law, but because of the prominence of legislation, these systems resemble the civil law tradition. They include Scandinavian countries, which inhabit an unusual place in the 'Romano-Germanic' family.

Religious law

No legal system can be properly understood without investigating its religious roots. These roots are often both deep and durable. Indeed, the Roman Catholic Church has the longest, continuously operating legal system in the Western world. The influence of religion is palpable in the case of Western legal systems:

> [B]asic institutions, concepts, and values...have their sources in
> religious rituals, liturgies, and doctrines of the eleventh and twelfth

centuries, reflecting new attitudes toward death, sin, punishment, forgiveness, and salvation, as well as new assumptions concerning the relationship of the divine to the human and of faith to reason.

In Europe in the 12th century, ecclesiastical law played an important role in a number of fields. Ecclesiastical courts claimed jurisdiction over a wide range of matters, including heresy, fornication, homosexuality, adultery, defamation, and perjury. Canon law still governs several churches, especially the Roman Catholic Church, the Eastern Orthodox Church, and the Anglican Communion of Churches.

The rise of secularism has not completely extinguished the impact of religious law. The jurisdiction of Western legislatures and courts over exclusively religious matters is frequently curtailed, and many legal systems incorporate religious law or delegate to religious institutions matters of a domestic nature. Nevertheless, one of the hallmarks of Western legality is the separation between church and state.

While a number of prominent religious legal traditions coexist with state systems of law, some have actually been adopted as state law. The most significant are Talmudic, Islamic, and Hindu law. All three derive their authority from a divine source: the exposition of religious doctrine as revealed in the Talmud, Koran, and Vedas respectively.

All have influenced secular law in a variety of ways. For example, Talmudic law (see Box 2) had a significant impact on Western commercial, civil, and criminal law. In addition to common and civil law systems, it is possible to identify four other significant legal traditions.

Islamic (or *sharia*) law (see Box 3) is based largely on the teachings of the Koran. It extends to all aspects of life, not merely those that pertain to the state or society. It is observed, to a greater

Box 2 Talmudic law

[The Talmud] represents a brilliant intellectual concept, a book of law which contains endless differences of opinion from all ages and dealing with all that had gone on before, while seen as never definitely finished and thus leaving room for still more opinion, as each age engages with it. There is no equivalent to it in any legal tradition.

H. Patrick Glenn, *On Common Laws*

Box 3 Islamic law

Islamic law...seeks constancy with common-sense assumptions about humanity, not through the refinement of categories of its own creation. [It] is a system of adjudication, of ethics and of logic that finds its touchstone not in the perfecting of doctrine, but in the standards of everyday life, and measured in this way it is enormously developed, integrated, logical and successful. Man's duty is to conform to God's moral limits, not to try to invent them. But within these limits established by God one can create relationships and traffic in the knowledge of their existence, intricacies and repercussions.

Lawrence Rosen, *The Anthropology of Justice: Law as Culture in Islamic Society*

or lesser extent, by more than one-fifth of the population of the world, some 1.3 billion people.

At its core, Hinduism postulates the notion of *karma*: goodness and evil on earth determine the nature of one's next existence. Hindu law (see Box 4), especially in relation to family law and succession, applies to around 900 million individuals, mostly living in India.

Customary law

To constitute custom, the practices involved require something
beyond mere usage or habit. They need to have a degree of legality.
This is not always easy to discern, though customary law
continues to play an important role, especially in jurisdictions
with mixed legal systems such as occur in several African
countries. The tenacity of custom is also evident in India and
China. Indeed, in respect of the latter, the Basic Law of the Special
Administrative Region of Hong Kong provides that customary
law, as part of the laws previously in force in Hong Kong (prior to
1 July 1997), shall be maintained. So, for example, legislation
provides that the courts may recognize and enforce Chinese
customs or customary rights in relation to land in the New
Territories.

Mixed legal systems

In some jurisdictions two or more systems interact. In South
Africa, for example, the existence of Roman-Dutch law is a
consequence of the influence of Dutch jurists who drew on Roman

law in their writing. This tradition was exported to the Cape Colony in the 17th and 18th centuries. The hybrid nature of South Africa's legal system is especially vivid, since, following the arrival of English common law in the 19th century, the two systems coexisted in a remarkable exercise of legal harmony. And they continue to do so:

> Like a jewel in a brooch, the Roman-Dutch law in South Africa today glitters in a setting that was made in England. Even if it were true (which it is not) that the whole of South African private law and criminal law had remained pure Roman-Dutch law, the South African legal system as a whole would still be a hybrid one, in which civil- and common-law elements jostle with each other.

This concoction is no longer nearly as effective in Sri Lanka or Guyana, to where Roman-Dutch law was exported in 1799 and 1803 respectively, but where the common law now predominates.

Chinese law

Traditional Chinese society, in common with other Confucian civilizations, did not develop a system of law founded by the ideas that underlie Western legal systems. Confucianism adopted the concept of '*li*': an intense opposition to any system of fixed rules that applied universally and equally. Though Chinese 'legalists' sought to undermine the political authority of this Confucian philosophy of persuasion by championing 'rule by law' ('*fa*') in place of the organic order of the Confucian '*li*', the latter continues to dominate China.

The spectacular modernization of China has generated a need for laws that facilitate its economic and financial development (see Box 5). But this new legalism has not been accompanied by an ideological partiality for law along Western lines. The role of law in modern China remains decidedly instrumental and pragmatic. Its system is essentially civilian and hence largely codified, but

Box 5 The future of the law in China

I would venture to suggest that as economic and social changes sweep through China as a result of the current economic reforms, the social context for the closed elements of traditional legal culture will, in the course of time, be replaced by a context more favourable to elements more consistent with liberalism, democracy, human rights, and the rule of law. They will thus find their place in a rejuvenated Chinese culture, which can and will continue to be informed and inspired by the open elements of the Chinese tradition, such as Confucian benevolence, moral self-cultivation, and the quiet but unending spiritual quest for harmony of 'heaven, earth, humanity and the myriad things'.

Albert H. Y. Chen, 'Confucian Legal Culture and its Modern Fate'

this has not yet engendered either greater esteem for the law or a diminution in the control of the Communist Party.

The allure of the law

Individuals aggrieved by iniquity often complain. 'There ought to be a law against that!' they cry. There is an understandable tendency to look to the law to resolve our problems. And the law's failure to provide a remedy may provoke a sense of frustration and anger. Yet legal regulation of antisocial behaviour is not as simple as it may appear, as should become clear when the challenges to the law of technology are considered in Chapter 6. Before we reach for the law, or a lawyer, it is worth recalling the words of the great American judge Learned Hand, who prescribed this antidote to an excessive faith in the law:

I often wonder whether we do not rest our hopes too much upon constitutions, upon laws and upon courts. These are false hopes; believe me, these are false hopes. Liberty lies in the hearts of men and women; when it dies there, no constitution, no law, no court can even do much to help it. While it lies there it needs no constitution, no law, no court to save it.

The validity or otherwise of this opinion should become evident in the course of these pages.

The functions of law

Football, chess, bridge are unthinkable without rules. A casual poker club could not function without an agreed set of rules by which its members are expected to abide. It is not surprising therefore that when they are formed into larger social groups, humans have always required laws. Without law, society is barely conceivable. We tend, unfortunately, towards selfishness. The restraint that law imposes on our liberty is the price we pay for living in a community. 'We are slaves of the law' wrote the great Roman lawyer Cicero, 'so that we may be free'. And the law has provided the security and self-determination that has, in large part, facilitated social and political advancement.

Order

The cliché 'law and order' is perhaps more accurately rendered 'law *for* order'. Without law, it is widely assumed, order would be unattainable. And order—or what is now popularly called 'security'—is a significant purpose of most governments. It is an essential prerequisite of a society that aspires to safeguard the well-being of its members.

Thomas Hobbes famously declared that in his natural state, prior to the social contract, the condition of man was 'solitary, poor, nasty, brutish and short', though more than one student has rendered this maxim as '...nasty, *British* and short'. Law and government are required, Hobbes argues, if we are to preserve order and security. We therefore need, by the social contract, to surrender our natural freedom in order to create an orderly society. His philosophy is nowadays regarded as somewhat authoritarian, placing order above justice. In particular, his theory, indeed his self-confessed purpose, is to undermine the legitimacy of revolutions against even malevolent governments.

He recognizes that we are fundamentally equal, mentally and physically: even the weakest has the strength to kill the strongest. This equality, he suggests, creates discord. We tend to quarrel, he argues, for three main reasons: competition (for limited supplies of material possessions), distrust, and glory (we remain hostile in order to preserve our powerful reputations). As a consequence of our inclination towards conflict, Hobbes concludes that we are in a natural state of continuous war of all against all, where no morals exist, and all live in perpetual fear. Order is, of course, only one part of the functions of law.

Justice

Though the law unquestionably protects order, it has another vital purpose. In the words of the 20th-century English judge Lord Denning:

> The law as I see it has two great objects: to preserve order and to do justice; and the two do not always coincide. Those whose training lies towards order, put certainty before justice; whereas those whose training lies toward the redress of grievances, put justice before certainty. The right solution lies in keeping the proper balance between the two.

The pursuit of justice must lie at the heart of any legal system. The virtual equation of law with justice has a long history. It is to be found in the writings of the Greek philosophers, in the Bible, and in the Roman Emperor Justinian's codification of the law. The quest for clarity in the analysis of the concept of justice has, however, not been unproblematic. Both Plato and Aristotle sought to illuminate its principal features. Indeed, Aristotle's approach remains the launching pad for most discussions of justice. He argues that justice consists in treating equals equally and 'unequals' unequally, in proportion to their inequality.

Acknowledging that the equality implied in justice could be either arithmetical (based on the identity of the persons concerned) or geometrical (based on maintaining the same proportion), Aristotle distinguishes between corrective or commutative justice, on the one hand, and distributive justice, on the other. The former is the justice of the courts which is applied in the redress of crimes or civil wrongs. It requires that all men are to be treated equally. The latter (distributive justice), he argues, concerns giving each according to his desert or merit. This, in Aristotle's view, is principally the concern of the legislator.

In his celebrated book, *The Concept of Law*, H. L. A. Hart maintains that the idea of justice:

> consists of two parts: a uniform or constant feature, summarised in the precept 'Treat like cases alike' and a shifting or varying criterion used in determining when, for any given purpose, cases are alike or different.

He contends that in the modern world the principle that human beings are entitled to be treated alike has become so well established that racial discrimination is usually defended on the ground that those discriminated against are not 'fully human'.

An especially influential theory of justice is utilitarianism, which is always associated with the famous English philosopher and law reformer Jeremy Bentham. In his characteristically animated language:

> Nature has placed mankind under the governance of two sovereign masters, *pain* and *pleasure*. It is for them alone to point out what we ought to do, as well as to determine what we shall do. On the

one hand the standard of right and wrong, on the other the chain of causes and effects, are fastened to their throne.... The *principle of utility* recognizes this subjection, and assumes it for the foundation of that system, the object of which is to rear the fabric of felicity by the hands of reason and of law. Systems which attempt to question it, deal in sounds instead of sense, in caprice instead of reason, in darkness instead of light.

To this end, Bentham formulated a 'felicific calculus' by which to assess the 'happiness factor' of any action.

There are numerous competing approaches to the meaning of justice, including those that echo Hobbes's social contract. A modern version is to be found in the important writings of John Rawls who, in rejecting utilitarianism, advances the idea of justice as fairness which seeks to arrive at objective principles of justice that would hypothetically be agreed upon by individuals who, under a veil of ignorance, do not know to which sex, class, religion, or social position they belong. Participants are required to imagine how each social class will be treated. None has any idea whether they are clever or dim, strong or weak. Nor do they know in which country or in what period they are living. They possess only certain elementary knowledge about the laws of science and psychology. In this state of blissful ignorance, they must unanimously decide upon a contract the general principles of which will define the terms under which they will live as a society. And, in doing so, they are moved by rational self-interest: each individual seeks those principles which will give him or her the best chance of attaining his chosen conception of the good life, whatever that happens to be.

Justice is unlikely to be attained by a legal system unless its rules are, as far as possible, reasonable, general, equal, predictable, and certain. None of these objectives can be achieved in absolute terms; they are ideals. So, for example, the law can never be utterly certain. Occasionally the facts of a case are obscure and difficult to discover. Similarly, the law itself may not be easy to establish—especially for the non-lawyer faced with a profusion of statutes, decisions of the courts, by-laws, and so on. The Internet has rendered the task of finding the law easier, but, in the face of an escalating spate of legal sources, it remains a formidable challenge. The maxim 'hard cases make bad law' expresses the important principle that it is better that the law be certain than that it be bent to accommodate an unusual case.

Justice requires more than just laws; the process whereby justice is attained must be a fair one. This entails, first, an impartial, independent judicial system (discussed in Chapter 5). Second, there must be a competent and independent legal profession (also discussed in Chapter 5). Third, procedural justice is a vital ingredient of a just legal system. This necessitates, among other things, access to legal advice, assistance and representation, and the guarantee of a fair trial (discussed in Chapter 4).

In a just or nearly just society, few obstacles beset the path of the judge who, in a general sense, seeks to advance the cause of justice. Heroism is rarely required. Where injustice pervades the legal system, however, the role of judge assumes a considerably more intractable form. How could a decent, moral, fair-minded person in a society such as Nazi Germany or apartheid South Africa square his conscience with his calling? This moral quandary is perhaps also encountered by ordinary individuals who inhabit an unjust society. Should the fact that the judge is a public official distinguish him from others who participate in the legal system or who simply derive benefit from its injustice? Are there compelling reasons for morally differentiating judges from others, particularly lawyers? The virtuous judge attempts to do justice when he can, admitting that his autonomy is curtailed in several major areas of the law. But is a conscientious lawyer not in the same boat? He or she strives to do good, often at great personal cost, within the strictures of the legal system. Do they not also lend legitimacy to the system? Is the moral dilemma not the same?

There are no simple answers to this sort of predicament. Institutionally, judges differ from lawyers: they are officers appointed or elected to implement the law. Their legal duty is plain. Lawyers, on the other hand, are not state officials. They owe a strong duty to their clients. They must, of course, work within the system, but their responsibility is to utilize the law, not to dispense justice. They may find the law morally repugnant, but their role within an unjust legal system is easier to justify than that of the judge. So, for example, lawyers in apartheid South Africa themselves recognized this distinction, and several prominent senior lawyers declared that on grounds of conscience they would decline appointment to the bench. Yet they continued as lawyers. And, though the temptation to withdraw from the system was often powerful, many lawyers played a courageous, sometimes heroic, part in the struggle for justice.

A lawyer may, however, decide that his or her participation in the legal system serves to legitimate it. This is a perfectly proper moral response. But it does not follow that the dilemma is therefore the same as for the state official. This is because of the important functional differences between the two. In particular, lawyers, unlike judges, are not concerned exclusively with the forensic process. Indeed, lawyers do some of their most worthwhile work when they advise clients of their rights, whether or not litigation is intended or anticipated (see Chapter 5). Thus, while appearance before the court may be regarded as a more palpable acceptance of its legitimacy, advising clients may not.

The law lays down certain ground rules. Murder is wrong. So is theft. Legal rules against these and other forms of antisocial behaviour are the most obvious, and the most conspicuous, instances of legal regulation. Modern governments seek to persuade us to behave well by means other than compulsion. Often the carrot replaces the stick. Advertising campaigns, official websites, and other forms of public relations exercises exhort us to do X or avoid Y. But by setting standards of conduct, the law remains the most powerful tool in the hands of the state.

Further, the law establishes a framework within which unavoidable disputes may be resolved. Courts are the principal forum for the resolution of conflict. Almost every legal system includes courts or court-like bodies with the power to adjudicate impartially upon a dispute and, following a recognized procedure, to issue an authoritative judgment based on the law.

The law facilitates, often even encourages, certain social and economic arrangements. It provides the rules to enable parties to enter into the contract of marriage or employment or purchase and sale. Company law, inheritance law, and property law all furnish the means by which we are able to pursue the countless activities that constitute social life.

Another major function of the law is the protection of property. Rules identify who owns what, and this, in turn, determines who has the strongest right or claim to things. Not only does the law thereby secure the independence of individuals, it also encourages them to be more productive and creative (generating new ideas that may be transformed into intellectual property, protected by patents and copyright).

The law also seeks to protect the general well-being of the community. Instead of individuals being compelled to fend for themselves, the law oversees or coordinates public services that would be beyond the capacity of citizens or the private sector to achieve, such as defence or national security.

Another dimension of the law that has assumed enormous proportions in recent years is the protection of individual rights.

For example, the law of many countries includes a bill of rights as a means of seeking to protect individuals against the violation of an inventory of rights that are considered fundamental. In some cases a bill of rights is constitutionally entrenched. Entrenchment is a device which protects the bill of rights, placing it beyond the reach of simple legislative amendment. In other jurisdictions, rights are less secure when they are safeguarded by ordinary statutes that may be repealed like any other law. Almost every Western country (with the conspicuous exception of Australia) boasts a constitutional or legislative bill of rights. The subject of human rights is discussed in Chapter 6.

The sources of law

Unlike manna, the law does not fall from the sky. It springs from recognized 'sources'. This reflects the idea that in the absence of some authoritative source, a rule that purports to be a law will not be accepted as a law. Lawyers therefore speak of 'authority'. 'What', a judge may ask a lawyer presenting an argument before her, 'is your authority for that proposition?' In reply, the common lawyer is likely to cite either a previous decision of a court or a statute. A civil lawyer will refer the court to an article of, say, the civil code. In either case, the existence of an acknowledged source will be decisive in the formulation of a legal argument.

In addition to these two conventional sources of law, it is not uncommon for the writings of legal academics to be recognized as authoritative sources of law. There are also certain sources that are, strictly speaking, non-legal, including (though it may be hard to believe) common sense and moral values.

Legislation

The stereotypical source of law in contemporary legal systems is the statute enacted by a legislative body that seeks to introduce new rules, or to amend old ones—generally in the name of reform, progress, or the alleged improvement of our lives. Legislation is, however, of quite recent origin. The 20th century witnessed an eruption of legislative energy by lawmakers who frequently owe their election to a manifesto of promises that presumes the existence of an unrelenting statutory assembly line. In most advanced societies, it is not easy to think of any sphere of life untouched by the dedication of legislators to manage what we may or may not do.

Statutes are rarely a panacea; indeed, they not infrequently achieve the precise opposite of what their draftsmen intended. Moreover, language is seldom adequately lucid or precise not to require interpretation. The words of a statute are rarely conclusive; they are susceptible of different construction—especially where lawyers are concerned. Inevitably, therefore, it falls to judges to construe the meaning of statutes. And when they do so, they normally create precedents that provide guidance for courts that may be faced with the interpretation of the legislation in the future.

A number of technical 'rules' have developed to assist judges to decode the intention of lawmakers. A classic example that demonstrates the various approaches to the legislative interpretation is a hypothetical statute that prohibits 'vehicles' from entering the park. This plainly includes a motor car, but what about a bicycle? Or a skateboard? One solution is to adopt the so-called 'literal' or 'textual' approach which accords the text in question its ordinary everyday meaning. Thus the definition of a 'vehicle' would not extend beyond an automobile, a truck, or a bus; bicycles and skateboards are not, in any ordinary sense, vehicles. Where, however, the plain meaning gives rise to an absurd result, its proponents concede that the approach runs into trouble, and the words or phrases in issue will need to be interpreted in a manner that avoids obvious illogicality.

A second approach seeks to discover the *purpose* of the legislation. In our example, we may conclude that the purpose of the provision is to secure the peace and quiet of the park. If so, we are likely to find it easier to decide what is the real intention of the legislation, and hence to distinguish between a car (noisy) and a bicycle (quiet). This approach also permits judges to consider the wider purposes of the legal system. Where either the narrow or broader purpose suggests an interpretation different from the literal meaning of the language, the purposive approach would prefer a liberal to a literal interpretation.

It is an approach that holds sway in several jurisdictions. Courts in the United States routinely scrutinize the legislative history of statutes in order to resolve ambiguity or confirm their plain meaning. A similar approach is evident in Canada and Australia. And under the European Communities Act of 1972, a court is required to adopt a purposive approach in construing legislation that implements European Community (EC) law. Indeed, since EC legislation tends to be drafted along civil law lines—expressed in fewer words than common law statutes, but with a high degree of abstraction—a purposive approach is unavoidable, and broad social and economic objectives are frequently considered by the courts. The European Court of Justice also tends to favour a purposive approach.

It is fair to say that there is no single best approach to unlock the door to an ideal construction of a statute. Indeed, there is considerable doubt as to whether the 'rules' are, or can be, uniformly applied. No less a distinguished author on statutory interpretation than Professor Sir Rupert Cross shared the doubts expressed by his Oxford pupils:

> Each and every pupil told me there were three rules—the literal rule, the golden rule and the mischief rule, and that the courts invoke which ever of them is believed to do justice in the particular case. I had, and still have, my doubts, but what was most disconcerting was the fact that whatever question I put to pupils or examinees elicited the same reply. Even if the question was What is meant by 'the intention of Parliament?' or What are the principal

extrinsic aids to interpretation? Back came the answer as of yore: 'There are three rules of interpretation—the literal rule…'

Moreover, there are those who cynically contend that the rules simply justify solutions reached on wholly different grounds.

Another difficulty intrinsic to the legislative process is that lawmakers cannot be expected to predict the future. Legislation designed to achieve a specific objective may fail when a new situation arises. This is especially true when innovative technology materializes to confound the law. Some of the awkward challenges to the legislation on copyright or pornography posed by the rise of digital technology and the Internet are discussed in Chapter 6.

Common law

One normally associates the phrase 'common law' with *English* common law. But common laws, in the sense of laws other than those particular to a specific jurisdiction, largely in the form of legislation, are not peculiar to England and English-speaking former colonies. Numerous forms of common law have existed, and endure, in several European legal systems, including France, Italy, Germany, and Spain. They developed from Roman roots and achieved their commonality by indigenous reception instead of imposition. In England, however, the judge-driven common law tended to be defined in jurisdictional and remedial terms. But though the common laws of Europe (Germany, France) seem to have transmogrified into national laws, they are not dead. Despite the advent of codification and the doctrine of precedent these— non-English—common laws, though battered and bruised, still survive. And they circulate tirelessly through the veins of various legal systems.

In respect of the common law of England, and those many countries to which it has been exported, previous decisions of courts (judicial precedents) are a fundamental source of law. As already mentioned, the doctrine of precedent stipulates that the combination of the important facts and the outcome of earlier cases is generally binding on courts who subsequently hear similar cases. The idea is based on the principle '*stare decisis*' ('let the decision stand'). It is, of course, designed to promote the stability and predictability of the law, as well as ensuring that like cases are, as far as possible, treated alike.

Every common law jurisdiction has its distinctive hierarchy of courts, and the doctrine of precedent requires courts to follow the decisions of courts higher up the totem pole. In doing so, however, the lower court need follow only the *reasoning* employed by the higher tribunal in reaching its decision—the so-called *ratio decidendi*. Any other statements made by the judges are not binding: they are 'things said by the way' (*obiter dicta*). For example, a judge may give his opinion on the case, which is not relevant to the material facts. Or she may pontificate on the social context in which the case arose. In neither case need a subsequent judge regard these utterances as anything more than persuasive.

Discerning the *ratio decidendi* of a case is not infrequently an arduous journey through an impenetrable thicket of law and fact. Judgments may be long and convoluted. Where the court consists of several judges, each may adduce different reasons to arrive at the same conclusion. Though judges and academics have supplied various road maps, there is no easy route. A simple formula is not available to uncover the binding chunk of the judgment. As with much in life, it requires practice and experience.

The notion that previous decisions (often ancient) should determine the outcome of contemporary cases is occasionally ridiculed. Most famously, Jeremy Bentham stigmatized the doctrine of precedent in dyspeptic terms:

> [T]he more antique the precedent—that is to say, the more barbarous, inexperienced, and prejudice-led the race of men, by and

among whom the precedent was set—the more unlike that the same *past* state of things…is the *present* state of things.

It is frequently assumed that Continental systems of law do not employ an equivalent doctrine of precedent under which judges are bound to follow decisions of a higher court. This is mistaken. In practice, a judgment of the French Cour de Cassation or the German Bundesgerichtshof will be followed by lower courts no less than the judgment of a common law court of appeal. There is, however, a difference that stems largely from the importance civil law systems attach to legislation. The judgments of French courts, for example, are generally considerably shorter than those delivered by common law judges because they consider their task merely to interpret legislation rather than to offer the exhaustive analysis of the law that characterizes common law judicial decisions. That chore is usually left to legal scholars.

The judgments of German courts tend towards the more philosophical or doctrinal with less prominence given to the facts of the case. And judges attach greater significance to academic books and articles. Scandinavian jurisdictions seem to reside in the middle ground between the common law and the civilian approach in the operation of binding precedent.

Other sources

In a perfect world the law would be clear, certain, and comprehensible. The reality is some way from this utopian vision. Law in all jurisdictions is a dynamic organism subject to the vicissitudes of social, political, and moral values. One influential foundation of moral ideas has already been mentioned: natural law, the ancient philosophy that continues to shape the teachings of the Roman Catholic Church. As we saw, it proceeds from the assumption that there are principles that exist in the natural world that we, as rational beings, are capable of discovering by the exercise of reason. For instance, abortion is regarded as immoral on the ground that it offends natural law's respect for life.

In spite of the caricature of law, lawyers, and courts existing in an artificial, hermetically sealed bubble, judges do reach out into the real world and take account of public opinion. Indeed, on occasion courts respond with unseemly alacrity, such as when the media laments the alleged leniency of judges in a certain case, or in respect of a particularly egregious crime. Judges may react rashly (dare one say injudiciously?) by flexing their sentencing muscles apparently to placate perceived public opinion.

More prudently perhaps, courts, much to the gratification of academic lawyers, increasingly cite their scholarly colleagues' views as expressed in textbooks and learned journals. To be quoted by a judge is recognition, not only that one's works are read, but that they carry some weight with those who actually decide what the law is.

In the absence of direct authority on a point of law, courts may even permit lawyers to refer to 'common sense' to support an argument. This might include widely accepted notions of right and wrong, generalizations about social practices, fairness, perceptions of the law, and other common conceptions that cynics occasionally represent as foreign to the legal process. Indeed, a distinguished American judge famously declared:

> The life of the law has not been logic; it has been experience. The felt necessities of the time, the prevalent moral and political theories, intuitions of public policy, avowed or unconscious, even the prejudices which judges share with their fellow-men, have a good deal more to do than the syllogism in determining the rules by which men should be governed. The law embodies the story of a nation's development through many centuries, and it cannot be

dealt with as if it contained only the axioms and corollaries of a book of mathematics.

This observation may provide some reassurance to those who regard the law—and judges—as being out of touch with the lives of real people.

Chapter 2
Law's branches

The numerous branches of the law constantly multiply. As social life is transformed, the law is rarely far behind to invent and define new concepts and rules, and to resolve the disputes that inevitably arise. Thus our brave new legal world continues to usher in novel subjects: space law, sports law, Internet law, media law, and so on. At the core of most legal systems, however, are the fundamental disciplines that hark back to the roots of law: the law of contract, tort, criminal law, and the law of property. To that nucleus must be added a horde of disciplines, including constitutional and administrative law, family law, public and private international law, environmental law, company law, commercial law, social security law, competition law, the law of evidence, succession, insurance law, labour law, intellectual property law, tax law, securities law, banking law, maritime law, welfare law, media law, and human rights law. To facilitate criminal and civil trials and other practical matters (such as the conveyance of land, the drafting of wills), complex rules of procedure have developed, spawning their own subcategories. This chapter describes the most significant branches of law's vast and flourishing tree.

Public and private law

The distinction between public and private law is fundamental, especially to the civil law systems of Continental Europe and its former colonies. Though there is no general agreement as to precisely how or where the line should be drawn, it is fair to say that public law governs the relationship between citizen and state, while private law concerns that between individuals or groups in society. Thus, constitutional and administrative law is the archetypal example of public law, whereas the law of contract is one of many limbs of private law. Criminal law, since it largely involves prosecutions by the state against offenders, also belongs under the umbrella of public law. (All three branches are described later.) As the state intrudes more and more into our lives, however, the boundary between public and private law grows ever fuzzier.

Contract

Agreements are an indispensable element of social life. When you agree to meet me for a drink, borrow a book, or give me a lift to work, we have entered into an agreement. But the law will not compel you to turn up at the bar, return my book, or pick me up in your car. These social arrangements, while their breach may cause considerable inconvenience, distress, and even expense, fall short of a contract as understood by most legal systems.

One of the hallmarks of a free society is the autonomy it affords its members to strike the bargains of their choice, provided they do not harm others. Freedom of contract may also be defended on utilitarian grounds: by enforcing contracts in accordance with the value placed on things by the market, resources—goods and services—may be bought by those who place the highest value upon them. It is sometimes claimed that this yields a just distribution of scarce resources.

Those who champion the free market consider individuals to be the best judges of their own welfare. In the 19th century, especially in England, the law of contract, as the facilitator of the optimum relations of exchange, was developed to a high degree of sophistication (some would say mystification) in pursuit of this cardinal value of commercial and industrial life. It is certainly true that business is inconceivable without rules of contract, but there is an inescapable inequality of bargaining power in any society. In theory, my contract with the electricity company that supplies power to my home regards both parties as being on an equal footing. But this is simply not the case. I am hardly in a position to haggle over the terms of the agreement which is inevitably a standard-form contract. A featherweight is engaged in a contest with a squad of heavyweights. The law therefore often tempers the hardship of so-called 'unfair' terms by consumer legislation and other institutional means that attempt to redress the balance by, for instance, empowering courts to disallow unconscionable clauses and permitting them to enforce only 'reasonable' terms.

In order to constitute a *binding* contract, the law normally requires that the parties to the agreement actually *intend* to create legal relations. Breaking a promise is almost always regarded as immoral, yet it results in legal consequences only where certain requirements are satisfied, though in certain civil law countries (such as France, Germany, and Holland) a person may be held liable, even before his offer is accepted, for failing to negotiate in good faith.

The common law notionally dissects agreement into an offer by one party and an acceptance of that offer by the other. By making an offer the 'offeror' expresses—by word, speech, fax, email, or even by conduct—his readiness to be bound in contract when it is accepted by the person to whom the offer is addressed, the 'offeree'. Thus Adam advertises his car for sale for £1,000. Eve offers him £600. Adam replies that he will accept £700. This is a counter-offer, which Eve is obviously free to accept or reject. Should she accept, there is agreement and, provided the other legal requirements are satisfied, a binding contract. This analysis is a helpful method by which to determine whether agreement has actually taken place, but it is somewhat artificial; it is often difficult to say who is the offeror and who is the offeree. For example, final agreement may be preceded by protracted negotiations involving numerous proposals and counter-proposals by the parties. To describe the process as constituting offer and acceptance is something of a fiction.

Hundreds of cases have grappled with factual situations that do not fit neatly into an offer-and-acceptance paradigm. There is also the recurring difficulty of the extent to which, if at all, an offeror should be bound by his offer. The common law stipulates that until you accept my offer I am at liberty to withdraw it. German, Swiss, Greek, Austrian, and Portuguese law, on the other hand, provide that I am bound by my offer; I cannot simply revoke it with impunity. A purported withdrawal has no legal effect. French and Italian law adopts an intermediate position. Thus the Italian Civil Code provides that an offer may not be revoked before the expiry of a specified period. If no period is specified in the offer, it may be withdrawn before acceptance. But if the offeree has relied on the offer in good faith, he may claim damages for the financial loss he has incurred in preparing to perform his side of the bargain.

The common law requires evidence not only of a serious intention to be legally bound, but also what is known as 'consideration', a concept absent from civil law systems. Consideration is the bargain element of the agreement: each party stands to gain something from the agreement—otherwise they would not have entered into it. These elements are illustrated by the classic case of *Carlill v Carbolic Smoke Ball Company* in 1892. The Carbolic Smoke Ball Company advertised its product—a smoke ball that it claimed would protect the user from contracting influenza. It undertook to pay £100 to anyone who, after using the apparatus, caught the 'flu. The advertisement included the following statement:

£100 reward will be paid by the Carbolic Smoke Ball Company to any person who contracts the increasing epidemic influenza, colds or any disease caused by taking cold, after having used the ball three times daily for two weeks according to the printed directions supplied with each ball. £1000 is deposited with the Alliance Bank, Regent Street, shewing our sincerity in the matter.

Mrs Carlill, relying on this promise, purchased a ball and used it according to the instructions. She nevertheless contracted influenza. The company claimed that there was no enforceable contract between it and Mrs Carlill since their offer had not been accepted—she had not informed the company that she had accepted its offer. Nor, they argued, was there any consideration because the company had not received any benefit from a purchaser's use of the smoke ball once it had been sold.

Both arguments were rejected by the court. It held that the advertisement constituted an offer of a *unilateral* contract between the company and anyone who, having seen the advertisement, acted on it. (Normally, contracts are *bilateral*: they involve an exchange of promises between two parties.) In this case, however, since Mrs Carlill had satisfied the conditions, she was entitled to enforcement of the contract. Informing the company that she had used the ball formed part of the acceptance. Moreover, by depositing £1000 in the bank to 'show their sincerity in the matter' the company was plainly making a serious offer. In respect of consideration, the court ruled that Mrs Carlill's conduct constituted consideration for the promise to pay her the £100 reward (see Figure 4).

So, for example, suppose I agree to sell you my car; I stand to gain the purchase price and you, to acquire the ownership of the vehicle. If I ignore my agreement with you and sell my car to someone else, you may invoke the law to obtain a remedy—because you relied on my keeping my promise. This is known as breach of contract, which is discussed later.

In their general approach to contracts, there is unquestionably a divergence between the major systems of law. The common law is

4. Mrs Carlill, relying on the manufacturer's promise, purchased and used the smoke ball, but it did not prevent her catching influenza.

normally regarded as pragmatic and business-oriented, while the civil law tends to be more moralistic. It is nevertheless possible to postulate a number of general principles that are accepted, to a greater or lesser extent, by both legal systems.

It is usually the case that *social* agreements are not binding. As already described, our agreement to meet for a drink lacks the necessary intention to be bound in law. Nor will a court allow me to recover the expenses I incurred travelling to the bar where you promised that you would be waiting for me. The common law, as we saw, also requires that, in return for a promise, the promisee (me) must give 'consideration'. This may lead to absurd or unjust consequences. For example, in a famous English case two sailors jumped ship. The captain was unable to replace them so he promised the rest of the crew more money, but reneged on his undertaking. The sailors lost their claim for the extra wages because they were already bound by their contract to assume extra duties on board. They had given no new consideration in return for the captain's promise to increase their pay. Various technical means have been devised by courts, especially in the United States, to avoid this sort of injustice.

The parties must have the capacity to enter into a contract. Though they differ in detail, all legal systems control the extent to which their members have the competence to enter into contractual relations. In particular, the young (minors) or those afflicted by mental or other impairments of their rational faculties are generally regarded as incapable of binding themselves contractually.

Contrary to the popular myth, a contract does not generally need to be in writing. Apart from certain contracts (the sale of land is the most conspicuous example), no formality is required to bind the parties. An oral agreement is generally no less binding than a written one, though, as we have seen, the common law requires evidence of consideration in return for a promise. Increasing government paternalism—in the name of consumer protection—has, however, generated a rise in the number of formalities, including written, or more usually printed, contracts required by legislation.

Certain 'contracts' are void because they offend 'public policy'. The concept of freedom of contract notwithstanding, the law will not countenance agreements that seek to use the law to achieve immoral or unlawful objectives. They are likely to be struck down by courts as void. But social mores rarely stand still; what was considered immoral a century ago appears tame in today's permissive circumstances. For example, German courts once routinely negated a lease of premises for use as a brothel.

Mistake, misrepresentation, or duress may render a contract voidable. This is because there is, in effect, no genuine agreement. Under certain circumstances, therefore, the law may allow me to void the contract where there has been a mistake, misrepresentation, duress, or undue influence. For example, if I am mistaken as to the subject of the contract (I thought I was buying a Ferrari, but you were, in fact, selling a Ford), or you have misrepresented the Ford as a Ferrari, or you forced me into the sale, I have defences to your claim that I should perform my side of the agreement, and if I can show that there has been, say, fraudulent misrepresentation, the contract may be vitiated.

A court may award damages for breach of contract. Should I fail to perform my obligations under a contract, you may sue me to recover compensation or, in a limited number of cases, compel me to carry out my side of the bargain. If, however, I can show that circumstances have rendered performance impossible or that the purpose of the contract has been frustrated, I may escape liability for breach of contract.

Suppose I agree to rent you my villa for a week. You arrive at the door and I refuse to allow you to enter. I appear to have breached our contract and you may want to obtain compensation. But how much? Should the law attempt to place you in the position you were in before you entered into the contract with me? Or should it seek to restore you to the position you would have been in if the contract had been carried out? Or should I simply be required to return the deposit I took from you in order to secure your booking? What if I refused you access to the villa because a storm had rendered the electricity supply unsafe? Would it make a difference if the storm occurred a month ago or only yesterday?

These thorny questions have spawned a plethora of intricate judicial analysis in all the major legal systems. The solutions differ, occasionally significantly, but typically where a party's breach is completely outside of her control—natural disasters offer the best example—she may be released from her contractual obligations.

Tort

Torts (or delicts, as they are called in Continental legal systems) are civil wrongs. They include injuries to my person, property, reputation, privacy, even my peace of mind. Like the law of contract, the law of tort grants victims (or 'plaintiffs', now—oddly—called 'claimants' by English law) the right to obtain compensation for their loss. Unlike contract, however, which has as its principal goal the keeping of promises, tort law protects a wide range of interests. The law provides remedies, pre-emptive and compensatory, for conduct that causes harm either intentionally or negligently. The latter have become the principal focus of modern tort law. Accidents will happen, but where they are the consequence of your negligence, I may be able to recover damages to recompense my loss. So, for example, should you run me over in your car, and I can prove that you were driving negligently, I may be awarded damages to cover the cost of my hospital treatment, the money I lost through being away from work, and my pain and suffering.

To succeed, the plaintiff normally has to prove that the wrong was done intentionally or negligently. Most torts are actionable only when they have caused actual injury or damage, though certain torts whose principal purpose is to protect rights rather than to compensate for damage (such as trespass) are actionable without proof of damage. The defendant (also known as the tortfeasor in common law systems) is normally the person who is primarily liable, though, according to the rules of vicarious liability, one person (e.g. an employer) may be held liable for a tort committed by another person (e.g. an employee).

Torts may also sometimes be breaches of contract. For example, the negligent driver of a bus who causes injury to his passengers has committed both the tort of negligence and a breach of the contract to carry the passengers safely to their destinations.

They may recover damages either in tort or for breach of contract, or both. The bus driver may also have committed a crime (e.g. dangerous driving).

While the protection of the interests in property and bodily security are reasonably straightforward, the courts of many jurisdictions have encountered difficulties when it comes to compensating victims whose loss is not physical, but either purely economic, or emotional. Suppose, as occurred in an English case, the defendants negligently damage an electrical cable while carrying out construction work near the plaintiff's factory. As a result, the production is severely harmed and the plaintiff suffers financial loss. The physical loss (the damage to the materials) was clearly recoverable, but since the cable was not the plaintiff's property the loss was 'purely economic'. Can he recoup it? The common law, after some twists and turns by English courts, answers in the negative. The fear seems to be that allowing recovery will open the floodgates of litigation, a frequent concern expressed by judges, especially in England. In France, on the other hand, no distinction is drawn between physical and economic loss.

Comparable judicial trepidation attends the question of emotional distress. Where the injury consists of psychiatric illness as a result of physical harm, the courts look for some degree of 'proximity' between the plaintiff and the victim. The complexity of this calculation is tragically illustrated by a House of Lords decision in 1992. A crush in a sports stadium resulted in the death of ninety-five football fans, and more than 400 were injured. The police acknowledged their negligence in allowing too many spectators into an already overcrowded ground. The match was to have been televised live. In the event, vivid images of the disaster were broadcast. The disturbing pictures were seen by some of the plaintiffs who knew that their friends or family were present in the stadium. Two of the plaintiffs were spectators in the ground, but not in the stands where the disaster occurred; the other plaintiffs learned of the disaster through radio or television broadcasts. All the plaintiffs lost, or feared they might have lost, a relative or friend in the calamity. They failed in their claim for compensation for emotional distress because they did not satisfy one or other of the control mechanisms used by the law when damages for psychiatric injury are claimed by plaintiffs who were not directly threatened by the accident but learned of it through sight or hearing. These limiting factors, the court held, are:

1. There must be a close tie of love and affection between the plaintiff and the victim.

2. The plaintiff must have been present at the accident or its immediate aftermath.

3. The psychiatric injury must have been caused by direct perception of the accident or its immediate aftermath and not by hearing about it from somebody else.

This requirement of 'proximity', as well as the other tests, have attracted considerable criticism, and calls for reform of the law in some jurisdictions. Problems also arise in circumstances where the injury falls short of a recognized mental affliction, and consists of the grief and distress that normally attends the loss of or injury to a loved one.

The law of tort not only attempts to recompense victims, it also seeks to deter persons from engaging in conduct that may injure others. Furthermore, it is said to 'shift' or 'distribute' the losses incurred in the case of negligent injury. To put the matter simply, where you are at fault in causing my injury, the law transfers the loss to you. Why should I have to bear the loss that you have negligently caused? You will see at once that this apparently simple question conceals a host of difficult issues about the nature of negligence: what is 'fault', what constitutes a 'cause', and so on. In the modern world dominated by insurance, the issue tends to alter from blame to burden: instead of asking 'who is at fault?' the question becomes 'who can best bear the cost?' And the answer is often the insurance company, with whom there is normally a compulsory liability insurance policy.

The common law of torts is a veritable cornucopia of wrongs. It includes trespass to land, trespass to person (which includes assault and battery), nuisance, defamation, and breach of statutory duty. But, as mentioned, in practice they are eclipsed by the tort of negligence, which is based on the fault principle. The plaintiff must prove that the defendant owed him a *duty of care* which was breached by his failure to live up to the standard of 'the reasonable man', thereby *causing* the plaintiff injury or damage.

Each of these three elements requires brief elaboration. The duty of care was vividly encapsulated in one of the most celebrated judicial pronouncements in all of the common law. In the landmark case of *Donoghue v Stevenson*, Mrs Donoghue complained of finding a snail in a ginger beer bottle, but the judgment was considerably more portentous.

The precise facts of the case have never been clearly established, but it appears that Mrs Donoghue accompanied her friend to a café in the Scottish town of Paisley (see Figure 5). Her friend ordered drinks. The café owner poured some of the contents of a bottle of ginger beer into a glass containing ice cream. Mrs Donoghue drank some of the contents and her friend lifted the bottle to pour the remainder of the ginger beer into the glass. Allegedly, a decomposed snail floated out of the bottle into the glass. Mrs Donoghue subsequently complained of stomach pain, and her doctor diagnosed her as having gastroenteritis. She also claimed to have suffered emotional distress as a result of the incident. The law of tort did not then permit a victim in a situation such as hers to sue the café owner. Nevertheless, the House of Lords held that a plaintiff in the position of Mrs Donoghue was owed a duty of care by a manufacturer like Stevenson who had made the ginger beer. Drawing on the biblical injunction

5. The alleged snail in Mrs Donoghue's ginger beer launched a new form of liability based on a manufacturer's duty of care.

that one has a duty to love one's neighbour, Lord Atkin famously declared:

> The rule that you are to love your neighbour becomes in law you must not injure your neighbour; and the lawyer's question: Who is my neighbour? receives a restricted reply. You must take reasonable care to avoid acts or omissions which you can reasonably foresee would be likely to injure your neighbour. Who, then, in law, is my neighbour? The answer seems to be—persons who are so closely and directly affected by my act that I ought reasonably to have them in contemplation as being so affected when I am directing my mind to the acts or omissions that are called in question.

In other words, you owe a duty to persons whom it is foreseeable are likely to be harmed by your conduct. The standard of care is therefore an *objective* one: you are judged by reference to the reasonable man. So, for example, an English court decided that the standard of care expected of a learner driver was the same as any other driver of a motor vehicle.

Finally, as a matter of fact the defendant must cause the plaintiff's loss. The question of causation has exercised the mind of many a common law judge; concepts such as 'remoteness of damage' and 'proximate cause' seem frequently to obscure what is ultimately a policy decision by the court as to what it considers to be fair or in the best interests of society.

The reasonable man—the hypothetical person against whom a defendant's conduct is measured—is frequently described as 'the man on the Clapham omnibus' (see Box 6), though in an examination one of my students (relying, I suppose, on my spoken words rather than consulting those of the judge) preferred to render the phrase: 'the man on the clapped-out omnibus'!

A similar approach is evident in the equally legendary American case of *MacPherson v Buick Motor Co.* in which Justice Cardozo held that where a manufacturer negligently produces a defective car that injures the person who purchased it from the dealer, the manufacturer is liable to that person despite the absence of a contract between them and the person injured.

The plaintiff in a negligence action is required to prove that the defendant's conduct actually *caused* his injury or damage. It is often the case, however, that the relationship between cause and effect is too remote. This question has proved remarkably complex and has generated a vast body of case law, especially in England.

It is not always clear whether in order to be held liable the defendant must reasonably foresee the *precise* type of damage that results from his negligence. Nor is it certain that he will be held responsible for damage that is more extensive or that occurs in an atypical manner. The courts tend, on the whole, to decide these intractable cases on policy grounds.

To the plaintiff's claim that the defendant negligently caused his loss, the defendant may raise a number of defences, including that the plaintiff voluntarily accepted the risk by, say, accepting a lift from a seriously drunk driver. Or the defendant might argue that the plaintiff was himself negligent and therefore contributed to his injury by failing to notice that the driver was dangerously inebriated.

Certain special circumstances may, however, dictate that a defendant be held responsible regardless of whether she is at fault. This is known as 'strict liability'. The protection of public health or safety militates against the fault principle, especially where the defendant is engaged in an inherently dangerous activity such as the use of explosives. Liability is often perceived as the price to be paid in return for the profits made by large corporations that indulge in potentially harmful activities.

The French Civil Code is fairly sweeping in this respect. It imposes strict liability for the things 'which one has under one's control'. A 'thing' includes any corporeal object whether it consists of a gas, a fluid, electric cables, or radioactive materials. Motor vehicles are things. Italian law renders the driver of a vehicle strictly liable, unless he did everything possible to avoid the accident. German law imposes strict liability on the driver of a vehicle who causes bodily injury or property damage, as well as on railway, gas, and electricity companies.

Anglo-American law finds the concept of strict liability less congenial, though under the so-called 'rule in *Rylands v Fletcher*' a defendant who brings on to his land a source of danger is strictly liable should it 'escape' and cause damage. The rule has been applied, among other hazards, to fire, gas, water, chemicals, fumes, electricity, and explosions. Strict liability may also arise under statute for harm caused by animals. An employer may also be held strictly liable for the acts of an employee in the course of his employment ('vicarious liability').

The difficulty of proving negligence by manufacturers has led to the considerable growth, especially in the United States, of a form of strict liability known as 'products liability'. The consumer is rarely able to check whether the car he buys is free of defects. The law therefore provides that if a product is defective at the time the defendant put it into circulation, the plaintiff need not prove negligence.

Another recent, predominantly American, development is the emergence of so-called 'mass torts'. These are lawsuits launched by a large number of plaintiffs ('class actions') associated with a single product. They include product liability claims against, for example, tobacco companies for lung cancer caused by smoking, injuries caused by breast implants, and large-scale, 'man-made' disasters such as aeroplane crashes and explosions at chemical plants.

The costs, delays, and injustices of the fault principle have generated deep dissatisfaction with the tort system of compensating accident victims. This has become so widespread and pervasive that cynicism greets the attempts by the rapidly declining number of fault-based stalwarts who attempt to defend its continuation. The only members of society who profit from the system, it is alleged, are the lawyers. Some jurisdictions (notably New Zealand and Quebec) have introduced comprehensive systems of no-fault insurance under which the law of tort is abolished for personal injury caused by accident. Victims of accidents are compensated from special funds created for this purpose. Detractors question the consequence of this munificence on the deterrent effect of a fault-based system, though it is widely acknowledged that, especially in the case of traffic accidents, compulsory insurance policies are the death knell of tort law.

In addition to wrongs committed negligently, the law recognizes a number of intentional torts or delicts. Among them is the civil wrong of defamation. The classic (rather technical) definition of the common law tort of defamation is that the wrong consists in publishing a false statement about the plaintiff which tends to lower him or her in the estimation of right-thinking members of the community generally, or which tends to cause him or her to be shunned or avoided, or which brings him or her into hatred, ridicule, or contempt, or which tends to discredit him or her in his or her trade or profession.

The test is an objective one; the fact that the defendant did not intend to defame the plaintiff is not a relevant consideration. Nor does it matter that he was unaware of the circumstances which rendered an apparently innocuous statement defamatory, or that the statement is not believed to be true by anyone who reads it. The defendant may be held liable for the repetition of defamatory statements where he authorizes or intends such repetition, but, as a general rule, he is not liable for unauthorized repetition unless the person to whom it was published was under a duty to repeat it. Therefore in the case of a book, several publications normally occur: the author to the publisher; the author and publisher jointly to the printer; by the author, publisher, and printer jointly to the distributor; and so on. Each repetition is a new publication which gives rise to a new course of action. The law does, however, distinguish between those who are mere distributors, on the one hand, and those who take an active part in the production of the work, on the other. Similar questions arise in respect of the publishing of a libel on the Internet.

There are four main defences to an action for defamation. First is the defence of justification (or 'truth'). Acknowledging the significance of free speech, the law provides that it is a complete answer to an action for defamation for the defendant to prove that the statement he published is substantially true. Second, the defence of absolute privilege protects defamatory statements when made in the course of legislative, judicial, and other official proceedings. Third, the defence of qualified privilege obtains in circumstances where the defendant has a duty (legal, social, or moral) to make a statement to a person who has a corresponding interest or duty to receive it, i.e. where the publisher and those to whom the publication is made have a common interest in the data concerned. The defence extends to fair and accurate reports of legislative and judicial proceedings. Fourth, there is the defence of fair comment which, in practice, tends to be the most important. This defence protects honest expressions of opinion on matters of public interest and is particularly relevant to the protection of free speech—a fact recognized by the courts. The comment must be on a matter of public interest.

Matters of public interest have been held to include the public conduct of persons who hold or seek a public office or position of public trust, the administration of justice, political and state matters, the management of public institutions, works of art, public performances, and anything that invites comment or challenges public attention. But the statement must be one of opinion not fact. This is a distinction that is easier to draw in theory than in practice. It must be 'fair', that is, it must be based on facts, and supported by those facts; there must be a basis of fact sufficient to warrant the comment made. The facts upon which the comment is based must be true. If they are true and the defendant is honestly expressing his genuine opinion on a subject of public interest, then it does not matter whether a reasonable person would hold such an opinion.

The plaintiff may defeat the defence by proving that the defendant was actuated by malice. It is for the plaintiff to prove malice. Malice also defeats the defence of qualified privilege. In respect of fair comment, malice denotes any improper motive which may have caused the defendant to make his comment. In this sense, then, his comment is not an honest expression of his view. As a general rule, the test is 'Did the defendant believe the statement to be true?'

As mentioned before, the publication of defamatory material online has spawned a host of questions about both liability and defences. In the recently enacted Defamation Act in England, special provisions apply to an action brought against the operator of a website in regard to a statement posted on the website. A defence now exists if the operator can demonstrate that he did not post the offending statement on the site. But this defence may be defeated if the plaintiff can show that it is impossible for him to identify the person who posted the statement, that he gave the operator a notice of complaint in relation to the statement, and that the operator failed to respond to the notice of complaint.

Other legal systems adopt a different approach. In the United States, for example, the law is less sympathetic to plaintiffs as a result of the constitutional protection of free speech enshrined in the First Amendment. It is therefore very difficult for a public official to succeed in a defamation action; the 1964 landmark decision of the Supreme Court of *New York Times v Sullivan* held that public officials could recover damages for statements made about their public conduct only if the statements were made with 'actual malice'. This test is satisfied where the defendant knew the publication was untrue or did not know whether it was true or false, and was reckless with the truth as, for example, when they doubt the truth of a statement but do not bother to check its veracity before publishing it.

And civil law systems, rather than recognizing a separate tort of defamation, protect reputation under the wing of personality rights. In several respects, the approach in Germany, France, and other European countries is more stringent than the common law. For example, the defences such as fair comment and justification are often not available. Article 10 of the European Convention on Human Rights, which protects freedom of expression, has, however, tempered the harshness of the law. Most European countries also protect the plaintiff against 'insults', a potentially unlimited area of liability that has been criticized by the European Court of Human Rights. On the other hand, while awards of damages tend in common law courts to be high (sometimes exceptionally so), the fines imposed by European courts are relatively trifling.

Criminal law

Crime is irresistible—and not only to criminals. It is the stuff of popular culture. Think of the many, mostly American, movies such as *The Godfather, Taxi Driver, Pulp Fiction, Scarface, Reservoir Dogs*, and countless others, or the equally numerous television series portraying various aspects of crime and its detection and prosecution, including *Breaking Bad, The Wire, Law and Order, NYPD Blue, Hill Street Blues, The Sopranos*, and *Gomorrah*—to name only a few. We seem to revel in watching criminals both eluding and confronting criminal justice.

Typically, of course, criminal law punishes serious forms of antisocial behaviour: murder, theft, rape, blackmail, robbery, assault, and battery. Yet governments deploy the law to criminalize a host of minor forms of misbehaviour relating, in particular, to health and safety. These 'regulatory offences' occupy a sizeable proportion of modern criminal law. As with the law of tort, the concept of fault is central to the criminal law. Broadly speaking, most countries proscribe conduct that generates insecurity, causes offence, and harms the efficient operation of the government, the economy, or society in general.

Virtually every system of criminal law requires evidence of fault—intention or negligence—to convict a person of an offence. So, for example, the American Model Penal Code defines a crime as 'conduct that unjustifiably and inexcusably inflicts or threatens substantial harm to individual or public interests'. Criminal liability thus has three basic components: conduct, without justification, and without excuse. To amount to a crime, 'conduct' must inflict or threaten substantial harm to individual or public interests. In sum, therefore, criminal liability requires a person to engage in conduct that inflicts or threatens substantial harm to individual or public interests without justification and without excuse.

The criterion of 'harm' will differ according to the social and political values of each society, but all agree that conduct that impairs the security of the community or hurts the physical well-being or welfare of its members constitutes 'harm'.

Criminal responsibility normally entails the presence of a guilty act (the *actus reus*) as well as a guilty mind (*mens rea*). But these prerequisites will not ineluctably condemn the accused individual, for he may have one of several defences to excuse his otherwise criminal behaviour. Suppose I am attacked by a knife-wielding robber, and in the affray that ensues I slay my assailant. Provided I use 'reasonable force' to defend myself, I am entitled to a complete acquittal. The defence is, however, unlikely to excuse me killing to defend my property. Other defences include duress (where, for example, I am forced at the point of a gun to commit a crime), mistake (I genuinely believed the umbrella I took was mine), incapacity (the defendant is a child, too young to form the requisite *mens rea*), provocation, and insanity.

The traditional offences mentioned earlier are everywhere crimes, even though they are met with varying degrees of severity or form of punishment. In addition, society cannot tolerate attacks upon its own survival; treason, terrorism, and public disorder are therefore generally criminalized. Nor is the criminal law confined to these extreme assaults on the community; conduct that offends may attract the attention of the law where the affront or nuisance is sufficient: public nudity, excessive noise or odours, and prostitution are examples of conduct that may cross the threshold. And there is a tendency for criminal law to be utilized in pursuit of paternalistic ends. Think, for example, of laws requiring the wearing of seat belts or crash helmets, or the legislation in most countries prohibiting the possession of drugs. The ostensible purpose of these laws is to protect individuals against their own folly or fragility.

The common law requires that in order to convict the defendant his guilt must be proved 'beyond reasonable doubt'. Civil cases (such as an action for breach of contract or a tortious action for damages) relax the burden to one of 'a balance of probabilities'. The situation in respect of criminal trials in civilian legal systems is broadly the same, though the so-called 'inquisitorial' system obtaining in Continental Europe and other civil jurisdictions is often misunderstood, and the differences between the two approaches exaggerated.

As in tort, liability in the criminal law is occasionally strict, i.e. there are offences that can be committed without *mens rea*. Similarly, the rationale for this abandonment of fault is the protection of public welfare, for example, where a factory is held responsible for industrial pollution—despite the absence of negligence.

The prosecution must, of course, prove that the defendant did actually commit the offence with which he has been charged. Suppose we have a fight and I hit you on the head with a blunt instrument. You are rushed to hospital, where you are administered a drug that kills you. Am I guilty of your murder? Did I *cause* your death? Were it not for the wound I inflicted, you would not have been in the hospital that negligently administered the incorrect medication. But it is doubtful that any legal system would hold me responsible for your death.

Murder in most countries requires proof of the intention to kill ('malice aforethought' in the common law). Legal systems attempt, in a variety of ways, to classify homicide on the basis of the mental element involved. So, for example, the United States and Canada tend to distinguish between different types of killing that constitute murder. Thus, according to the Canadian Criminal Code, first-degree murder is the intentional, premeditated killing of another person or in the furtherance of another serious criminal offence such as robbery. Second-degree murder is the intentional killing of another person without premeditation (i.e. killing in the heat of the moment). Third, there is manslaughter, which is the killing of another person when there is no intent to kill. Fourth is infanticide—the killing of an infant while the mother is still recovering from the birth.

While liability for intentional killing is relatively uncontroversial, death caused by negligence is less straightforward, and the laws of various jurisdictions adopt different solutions to what is generally regarded as something of a quandary. Some require that the defendant *must have known*—subjectively—that his act may kill someone and that he nevertheless proceeds recklessly despite the risk. For example, I have been admonished never to point a loaded weapon at anyone. I ignore the warning, and the rifle I point towards you fires and you are killed. Other jurisdictions lack this prerequisite of knowledge and impose liability for negligent killing where the defendant acts with gross negligence. Still others require only ordinary negligence.

One of the primary functions of the criminal law is to authorize the punishment of convicted offenders. This may be justified on any of a number of (often competing) grounds. First, punishment is thought, sometimes correctly, to act as a deterrent both to the convict and to others. Few criminals, however, imagine they will be apprehended; the effectiveness of deterrence is thus questionable. Second, there are those who believe that through punishment, especially imprisonment, the offender will come to see the error of his ways and emerge a reformed individual. Unfortunately, the evidence in support of this benevolent attitude is meagre. It is argued, third, that the real purpose of punishment is retribution or desert: making the wrongdoer suffer for his crime: 'an eye for an eye'. An extreme contemporary example is Islamic *sharia* law, under which, according to most interpretations, the punishment for serious theft is the amputation of hands or feet (though for first offenders only one hand is cut off).

The state, by assuming responsibility for chastising the criminal, reduces the risk of victims of crime 'taking the law into their own hands'. Fourth, by locking up an offender, she is removed from society, thereby protecting the rest of us. Finally, especially in the case of minor offences, the criminal may be required to make amends through 'community service'. This form of punishment is then justified as a form of 'restorative justice'.

Of course, not every crime—even if the offender is apprehended results in a prosecution. The police and prosecutorial authorities exercise a discretion over which offences warrant the effort and expense of arrest, charge, and the application of the criminal justice system. Both will consider a range of factors, including the seriousness of the crime and the age and gender of the offender. Police discretion is especially evident in cases of domestic violence and traffic offences. An important benefit is that it gives officers a human face: it permits them, for instance, to offer young offenders a second chance, and it helps to enhance the public perception of the police. Deciding whether to launch a prosecution will depend on circumstances such as the sufficiency of evidence, the availability of alternatives, the offender's criminal record, and the extent to which he or she is willing to cooperate with the prosecution of others. The operation of discretion thus avoids inundating the criminal justice system with a deluge of cases. On the other hand, it is argued that excessive discretion can undermine the rule of law, particularly if it is exercised arbitrarily or inconsistently (say, in respect of celebrities).

Even after a prosecutor decides to indict a defendant, discretion may still be exercised. In many jurisdictions—most conspicuously in the US—a prosecutor may negotiate a 'plea bargain' under which a defendant pleads guilty in return for a reduction in the charge or a lighter sentence. Or the prosecutor may go further: he or she could enter a *nolle prosequi*, a formal statement by a prosecutor that a case is discontinued. This could be a result of inadequate or inadmissible evidence, false accusations, or the trivial nature the offence.

Property

Ownership is at the epicentre of social organization. The manner in which the law defines and protects this exclusive right is an important marker of the nature of society. And the law always has something to say on this subject, whether it is to confer absolute rights of private property, recognize collective rights, or adopt a position in between. Specifically, the law of property determines, first, what counts as 'property'; second, when a person acquires an exclusive right to a thing; and, third, the manner in which it protects this right.

To the first question there is general agreement that property includes land, buildings, and goods. The common law distinguishes between real property (land as distinct from personal or movable possessions) and personal property. Civil law systems distinguish between movable and immovable property. The former corresponds roughly to personal property, while immovable property corresponds to real property. But property is what the law declares it to be: a ten-dollar bill is a piece of paper with no intrinsic value; the law imparts value to it. In a similar fashion, the law may create property, as it does in the case of intellectual property (which includes copyright). As the owner of the copyright in this book, I have a monopoly of various rights over its copying and reproduction.

The second issue—who is the owner—is generally determined by discovering who has the strongest long-term right to control the thing in question. And this right will normally include the right to transfer ownership to another. In the case of land, however, I may not know whether the seller is the legal owner. Most legal systems therefore have some form of public land registration which enables prospective buyers to establish who the genuine owner is.

Third, the law may be called upon to settle a contest between the owner and the possessor of a thing. The former is, as we have seen, the person with the strongest long-term claim to the possession of a thing. But suppose I rent my villa to you for a year. You currently possess the property, and while I have an ultimate right to possess it, some legal systems favour the right of the tenant (at least for the duration of the lease) over the owner; others prefer the owner.

A significant branch of property law is the law of trusts, which developed out of the division in England between common law and a separate branch of the law known as 'equity', which developed in the 14th century as a result of dissatisfaction with the rigidity, corruption, and formalism of the common law. This led losing parties to petition the king to compel the other party to observe moral—rather than strictly legal—principles. The king conveyed these petitions to the lord chancellor, the chief administrative official, who, in time, came to adopt judicial powers, and the idea of equity was born. The inexorable conflict between the strict application of the law, on the one hand, and the principles of justice and morality, on the other, was well understood by Shakespeare who, in act IV scene 1 of *The Merchant of Venice*, has Portia declare:

> The quality of mercy is not strained
> It droppeth as the gentle rain from heaven
> Upon the place beneath. It is twice blest;
> It blesseth him that gives and him that takes.
> 'Tis mightiest in the mightiest; it becomes
> The thronèd monarch better than his crown.

Among the concepts to emerge from this equitable jurisdiction was the convenient institution of the trust, which is an arrangement by which a 'settlor' transfers property to one or more trustees who hold it for the benefit of one or more beneficiaries who have the right to enforce the trust in court.

Equity, rooted in conscience, also produced a number of important remedies, including the injunction. This enables a person to prevent in advance the commission of a legal wrong. For example, if I learn that you are about to publish an article defamatory of me, I may, in several jurisdictions, obtain an urgent injunction to stop you from doing so. Another equitable remedy is 'specific performance'. The common law allowed only the award of damages for breach of contract, but often the plaintiff seeks the performance of the contract rather than compensation. Since the 19th century, equity is applied in the same courts as the common law, and though the division between the two bodies of law lingers, equity has lost its mission as the 'compassionate female' in contrast to the common law's position as the 'inflexible male' (see Box 7).

Box 7 The Dickensian Court of Chancery

This is the Court of Chancery, which has its decaying houses and its blighted lands in every shire, which has its worn-out lunatic in every madhouse and its dead in every churchyard, which has its ruined suitor with his slipshod heels and threadbare dress borrowing and begging through the round of every man's acquaintance, which gives to monied might the means abundantly of wearying out the right, which so exhausts finances, patience, courage, hope, so overthrows the brain and breaks the heart, that there is not an honourable man among its practitioners who would not give—who does not often give—the warning, 'Suffer any wrong that can be done you rather than come here!'

Charles Dickens, *Bleak House*

Constitutional and administrative law

Whether or not it is in written form, every country has a constitution that specifies the composition and functions of the organs of government, and regulates the relationship between individuals and the state. Constitutional law analyses the extent to which the functions of government are distributed between the legislative, executive, and judicial branches of government: the 'separation of powers'.

Many constitutions incorporate a bill of rights that constrains the exercise of the power of government by conferring individual rights and freedoms on citizens. Such rights typically include freedom of speech, conscience, religion, the right of peaceful assembly, freedom of association, the right of privacy, equality before and equal protection of law, the right to life, the right to marry and found a family, freedom of movement, and the rights of persons charged with or convicted of a criminal offence.

Administrative law governs the exercise of the powers and duties by public officials. In particular, it concerns the control of such powers by the courts which, in many jurisdictions, increasingly engage in reviewing the exercise of legislation and administrative action. This has occurred largely as a consequence of the dramatic expansion over the last fifty years in the number of government agencies that regulate vast tracts of our social and economic lives. It also concerns the review of decisions made by so-called 'quasi-judicial' bodies, like professional disciplinary committees that affect the legal rights of their members. Their rulings are susceptible to 'judicial review' to determine whether they have acted reasonably.

The precise standard of reasonableness to be applied by the court differs in various common law jurisdictions. In the United States, for example, the court asks whether the body's decision was 'arbitrary or capricious' before deciding whether to strike it down.

The Canadian test is one of 'patent unreasonableness', while the Supreme Court of India deploys criteria of proportionality and legitimate expectation. English law adopts the standard known as '*Wednesbury* unreasonableness' (after a case of this name, in which it was held that a decision would be set aside if it 'is so unreasonable that no reasonable authority could ever have come to it').

In France, the Conseil Constitutionnel exercises exclusive judicial oversight, including in respect of legislation that fails to attract sufficient parliamentary support. It has the—unappealable—power to nullify the contested bill. The supreme courts (Conseil d'État and Cour de Cassation) seek to interpret the law in a manner consistent with the constitution. French administrative law recognizes certain *principes à valeur constitutionnelle* (principles of constitutional value), including human dignity, with which the executive must comply, even in the absence of specific legislative provisions to that effect. The German constitution (the Basic Law) guarantees judicial review as a check on the tyranny of the majority.

Several civil law countries have special administrative courts. Difficulties tend to arise in respect of determining whether a matter is one for these courts or belongs more properly in the ordinary courts. In France, for example, a special Tribunal of Conflicts decides where the matter should be heard, while in Germany the court in which the case is first pleaded determines whether it has jurisdiction and may transfer cases over which it denies jurisdiction. In Italy, the Court of Cassation is the ultimate authority when such conflicts arise.

Other branches

Family law relates to marriage (and its contemporary equivalents), divorce, children, child support, adoption, custody, guardianship, surrogacy, and domestic violence.

Public international law seeks to regulate the relations between sovereign states. These norms are generated by treaties and international agreements (such as the Geneva Conventions that comprise four treaties and three protocols governing the standards of international law in respect of the humanitarian conduct of war), the United Nations, and other international organizations, including the International Labour Organization, UNESCO, the World Trade Organization, and the International Monetary Fund.

The International Court of Justice (sometimes called the World Court), based in The Hague, was established in 1945 under the UN Charter in order to settle legal disputes between states and to issue advisory opinions on legal matters. The International Criminal Court was established in 2002 and also sits at The Hague. It hears prosecutions of alleged perpetrators of genocide, crimes against humanity, war crimes, and the crime of aggression. More than one hundred states are members of the court, but neither China nor the United States are among them; the latter expressing reservations about the ability of the court to respect the constitutional rights of American defendants (including trial by jury) and the prospect of the politicization of the court—fears that seem tenuous.

Environmental law is a patchwork of common law rules, legislation, and international agreements and conventions whose chief concern is to protect the natural environment against the depredations of humans, such as carbon emissions that cause pollution and probably global warming. It also seeks to promote 'sustainable development'.

Company law deals with the 'floating' of corporations and other business organizations. The concept of 'corporate personality' (under which a company has a distinct identity independent of its members) is of vital importance in the business world. It means that a company is a legal person with the capacity to enter into contracts, sue, and be sued. Company law also stipulates the rights and duties of directors and shareholders, and is increasingly concerned with rules of corporate governance, mergers, and acquisitions.

New branches of law are constantly burgeoning to keep pace with social, economic, and political developments and, of course, the relentless advance of technology. Some of these transformations are sketched in Chapter 6.

Chapter 3
Law and morality

Is torture wrong? What's wrong with abortion? Is homosexuality
sinful? Moral questions of this kind arise in almost any legal system.
And confronting them is among the fundamental characteristics
of a free society. Consider the recent landmark decision of the
United States Supreme Court declaring that the Constitution
guarantees a right to same-sex marriage.

Moreover, the language of morals is increasingly employed on
the international stage. When an American president described an
'axis of evil' existing between certain nations, he was (doubtless
unconsciously) presuming a normative yardstick by which to
measure the conduct of states that, since the formation of the
United Nations, is partly embodied in an expanding anthology of
international declarations and conventions.

Although we cannot easily evade moral question marks, the
identification, or even the acknowledgement, of moral values by
which to live is always contentious. Being or doing good is not
necessarily synonymous with obeying the law, even though the
law, its ideas, and its institutions, are often informed by moral
values. It would be strange if it were otherwise.

The relationship between the law and the moral practices (or
'positive morality') adopted by society may be represented by two

partially intersecting circles. Where they overlap we find a correspondence between the law and moral or ethical values (for example, murder is both morally and legally prohibited in all societies). Outside the overlapping zone, reside, on the one hand, acts which are legally wrong but not necessarily immoral (for example, exceeding your time on a parking meter) and, on the other, conduct which is immoral but not necessarily unlawful (such as adultery). The greater the intersection, the more likely the law is to be accepted and respected by members of that society.

In some cases, of course, there will be a conflict between the law and the moral code of certain individuals or groups. So, for example, a pacifist who is required to serve in the military may be compelled to become a conscientious objector and face imprisonment as a consequence of his violation of the law. Similarly, journalists in many countries claim a right not to disclose their sources. This will not, however, assist them when they are required to reveal this information as a witness in a trial.

More extreme is the situation in which the law actually *conflicts* with the majority's moral values. In apartheid South Africa, for instance, the law was used to pursue *immoral* aims. As the creation of a white minority, the political system disenfranchised every black person, and the law discriminated against them in several important aspects of social and economic life. In such cases, we are entitled to ask whether unjust legislation of this kind qualifies as 'law' at all. It raises the questions: must law be moral? Can anything count as law?

A celebrated, if somewhat inconclusive, debate between two leading legal philosophers sought to establish the grounds, if any, upon which immoral laws may nevertheless be regarded as 'law'. At its heart was a decision of a post-war West German court. In 1944, during Nazi rule, a woman who wished to dispose of her husband denounced him to the Gestapo for insulting remarks he had made about Hitler's conduct of the war. The husband was tried and sentenced to death, though his sentence was converted to service as a soldier on the Russian front. After the war the wife was prosecuted for procuring her husband's loss of liberty. Her defence was that he had committed an offence under a Nazi statute of 1934. The court nevertheless convicted her on the ground that the statute under which the husband had been punished offended the 'sound conscience and sense of justice of all decent human beings'.

H. L. A. Hart, Professor of Jurisprudence at Oxford, contended that the decision of the court, and similar cases pursuant to it, was wrong, because the Nazi law of 1934 was a formally valid law. Professor Lon Fuller of Harvard Law School, on the other hand, argued that, since Nazi 'law' deviated so significantly from morality, it failed procedurally to qualify as law. He therefore defended the court's decision, though both jurists express their preference for the enactment of retroactive legislation under which the woman could have been prosecuted.

For Fuller, law has an 'internal morality'. In his view, a legal system is the purposive human 'enterprise of subjecting human conduct to the guidance and control of general rules'. A legal system must conform to certain procedural standards, or what may appear to be a legal system is simply the bare exercise of state coercion. This 'inner morality of law' consists of eight essential principles, and failure to comply with any one of them, or substantial failure in respect of several, suggests that 'law' does not exist in that society. He relates the unhappy tale of a king, Rex, who, to his cost, neglects these eight principles. He fails to make rules at all, deciding questions on an ad hoc basis. He also fails to publicize the rules. He enacts rules which are retroactive, difficult to understand, contradictory, and which require conduct beyond the powers of the affected party. Moreover, his rules change so frequently that the subject cannot adjust his action by them. Finally, there is no correspondence between the rules as announced and their actual administration.

These failures are, Fuller explains, mirrored by eight forms of 'legal excellence' towards which a system of rules may aspire, and which are embodied in the 'inner morality of law'. They are generality, promulgation, non-retroactivity, clarity, non-contradiction, possibility of compliance, constancy, and congruence between declared rule and official action.

Where a system does not conform to any one of these principles, or fails substantially in respect of several, it could not be said that 'law' existed in that community. Thus, instead of adopting a substantive natural law approach, Fuller espouses a procedural natural law approach. (Natural law theory is discussed later in this chapter.) The 'internal morality of law' is essentially what Fuller calls a 'morality of aspiration'. Nor does it claim to accomplish any substantive ends, apart from the excellence of the law itself.

Not the law's business?

Professor Hart engaged in another important debate on the relationship between law and morality. This time his adversary was the English judge, Lord Devlin. The so-called Hart–Devlin debate illuminates certain fundamental aspects of the role of the law in seeking to enforce morality. It is a classic confrontation that remains a key launch pad for any serious discussion of this subject, not only in Britain but throughout the world.

The catalyst for the debate was a report in 1957 by a British committee, under the chairmanship of Sir John Wolfenden, appointed to examine the question of homosexual offences and prostitution. It concluded that the function of the criminal law was to preserve public order and decency, to protect citizens from what is offensive and injurious, and from exploitation and corruption of others, particularly those who are especially vulnerable: the young, the inexperienced, and the frail. But:

> Unless a deliberate attempt is to be made by society, acting through
> the agency of the law, to equate the sphere of crime with that of sin,
> there must remain a realm of private morality and immorality
> which is, in brief and crude terms, not the law's business.

In arriving at this conclusion (and recommending that both consensual homosexual acts between adults in private, and prostitution, should be decriminalized), the Wolfenden Committee was strongly influenced by the views of the 19th-century liberal utilitarian John Stuart Mill, who, in 1859, argued that:

> [T]he sole end for which mankind are warranted, individually or collectively, in interfering with the liberty of action of any of their number, is self-protection. The only purpose for which power can be rightfully exercised over any member of a civilized community, against his will, is to prevent harm to others. His own good, either physical or moral, is not a sufficient warrant.

At first blush, this 'harm principle' as the touchstone by which to fix the boundaries of the criminal law seems uncomplicated and attractive. But two immediate difficulties arise. First, is the criminal law not justified in punishing what another Victorian utilitarian, Sir James Fitzjames Stephen (uncle of the novelist Virginia Woolf), called 'the grosser forms of vice'? And, second, who is to say what constitutes 'harm'?

This pair of problems is the nub of the disagreement between Hart and Devlin. In a series of lectures in 1959, Lord Devlin took issue with the Wolfenden Committee's position, arguing that society has every right to punish conduct that, in the view of the ordinary member of society ('the man in the jury box'), is grossly immoral. Harm, he contended, is irrelevant; the fabric of society is maintained by a shared morality. This social cohesion is undermined when immoral acts are committed—even in private, and even if they harm no one. Societies disintegrate from within, he contended, more often than they are destroyed by external forces:

> There is disintegration when no common morality is observed and history shows that the loosening of moral bonds is often the first stage of disintegration, so that society is justified in taking the same steps to preserve its moral code as it does to preserve its

government…[T]he suppression of vice is as much the law's business as the suppression of subversive activities.

But, though Lord Devlin concedes that only those acts that cause 'intolerance, indignation and disgust' warrant punishment, Professor Hart challenges the very foundation of his 'social cohesion' argument. Surely, Hart insists, a society does not require a shared morality; pluralistic, multicultural societies may contain a variety of moral views. Moreover, even if there is a shared morality, is it obvious that its protection is essential to the survival of society? In respect of the first assertion, it does seem far-fetched to claim that a society's foundation is unable to withstand the challenge of a competing ideology or morality. Is a Western society gravely wounded by the Islamic prohibition of alcohol espoused by a significant proportion of its inhabitants? Equally, is an Islamic society unable to withstand the morality of a minority in its midst?

Hart does not, however, shrink from supporting a paternalistic role for the law. Differing with Mill, he acknowledges that there may be circumstances in which the law ought to protect individuals from physically harming themselves. The criminal law may therefore justifiably withhold the defence of consent to homicide and assault. Requiring seat belts in vehicles or crash helmets to be used by motorcyclists is a legitimate exercise of legal control.

A key distinction is also drawn by Hart between harm that is caused by public spectacle, on the one hand, and offence caused merely through knowledge, on the other. Hence bigamy may justifiably be punished since, as a public act, it may cause offence to religious sensitivities, whereas private consensual sexual acts by adults may cause offence—but only through knowledge, and thus do not justify punishment. Such acts may be best dealt with by legislation. In the words of the distinguished judge Lord Reid:

> Notoriously there are wide differences of opinion today as to how
> far the law ought to punish immoral acts which are not done in the

face of the public. Some think that the law already goes too far, some that it does not go far enough. Parliament is the proper place, and I am firmly of opinion the only proper place, to settle that. When there is sufficient support from public opinion, Parliament does not hesitate to intervene. Where Parliament fears to tread it is not for the courts to rush in.

A similar approach may be required in respect of the vexed question of how a woman's right to an abortion is to be reconciled with the moral position that regards the foetus as a person with a right to life.

A right to life?

The abortion debate in the United States is a compelling example of how moral questions can polarize a society. Christian groups condemn (occasionally violently) the practice of abortion, regarding it as murder. Feminists, on the other hand, consider the matter to be fundamental to a woman's right to control her own body. There is no apparent middle ground. Ronald Dworkin vividly portrays the ferocity of the struggle:

> The war between anti-abortion groups and their opponents is America's new version of the terrible seventeenth-century European civil wars of religion. Opposing armies march down streets or pack themselves into protests at abortion clinics, courthouses, and the White House, screaming at and spitting on and loathing one another. Abortion is tearing America apart.

At the core of the divisive subject of abortion is the decision of the United States Supreme Court in 1973 of *Roe v Wade* in which the court held, by a majority, that the abortion law of Texas was unconstitutional as a violation of the right to privacy. Under that law abortion was criminalized, except when performed to save the pregnant woman's life. The court held that states may prohibit abortion to protect the life of the foetus only in the third trimester.

6. The United States Supreme Court's momentous decision in *Roe v Wade* continues to engender fierce debate especially between feminists and pro-life advocates.

The decision, which Dworkin describes as 'undoubtedly the best-known case the United States Supreme Court has ever decided' is simultaneously embraced by feminists and denounced by many Christians. It is the—always vulnerable—slender thread by which the right of American women to a lawful abortion hangs (see Figure 6).

In the abortion debate the sanctity of human life has somehow to be morally weighed against the right of a woman over her body. Most European countries have sought to strike this balance by legislation that permits abortion within specified periods under certain prescribed conditions. In Britain, for example, abortion is lawful if it is certified by two medical practitioners that to continue the pregnancy would involve risk to the life of, or injury to, the pregnant woman or her existing children, and that the risk is greater than if the pregnancy were terminated. It is also lawful if there is a substantial risk that if the child were born it would suffer serious physical or mental handicap. It is a criminal offence to terminate a pregnancy when the child is capable of being born alive. This is normally after twenty-eight weeks. More recent legislation provides that a pregnancy that has not exceeded twenty-four weeks may be terminated where its continuation would involve risk, greater than if the pregnancy were terminated, of injury to the physical or mental health of the pregnant woman or any existing children of her family, but no time limit is imposed where termination may be necessary to prevent grave permanent injury to the physical or mental health of the pregnant woman, or risk to her life, or if there is a substantial risk that if the child were born it would suffer from such physical or mental abnormalities as to be seriously disabled.

In its quest for a conscientious resolution to this complex issue, each society must appraise its own moral currency (see Box 8). If, as most humans tend to believe, life is sacred, does a foetus count

Box 8 Moral inconsistencies?

Killing people outside war is the most seriously-regarded crime ordinarily committed. The only thing more strongly forbidden by our culture is eating people (even if they are already dead). We enjoy eating members of other species, however. Many of us shrink from judicial execution of even the most horrible human criminals, while we cheerfully countenance the shooting without trial of fairly mild animal pests. Indeed we kill members of other harmless species as a means of recreation and amusement. A human foetus, with no more human feeling than an amoeba, enjoys a reverence and legal protection far in excess of those granted to an adult chimpanzee. Yet the chimp feels and thinks...and may even be capable of learning a form of human language. The foetus belongs to our own species, and is instantly accorded special privileges and rights because of it.

Richard Dawkins, *The Selfish Gene*

as a person capable of suffering harm? If it does, how is ending its life to be distinguished from the humane killing of a living human? Should the welfare of the as yet unborn prevail over the distress suffered by a woman compelled to bear an unwanted pregnancy or endure the anxiety, cost, and difficulty of bringing up a disabled child?

A right to die?

Similar deliberation surrounds the equally daunting issue of euthanasia or 'mercy killing'. Doctors, lawyers, and ultimately courts perennially wrestle with the contentious question of an individual's 'right to die'. A distinction is usually drawn (not always convincingly) between active and passive euthanasia. The former entails the acceleration of a person's death by a positive act, such as an injection of potassium chloride. Most legal systems treat this as murder. The latter involves the shortening of life by an omission to act: a withdrawal of treatment, which is increasingly accepted by both the law and the medical profession in many jurisdictions as humane. But courts have not always found it easy to determine the lawfulness of withdrawing life support from an incurably or terminally ill patient who is in a persistent vegetative state (PVS), unable to make an autonomous decision.

Nor are generalizations easy in respect of either the morality or lawfulness of ending the life of a patient. There is, for instance, an important distinction between a patient who is incurable, and one who is terminally ill. The latter spectrum may range between incapacity (a fully conscious patient who can breathe unaided), artificial support (a fully conscious patient attached to a ventilator), unconsciousness, to intensive care (where the patient is comatose and is attached to a ventilator). Different considerations arise in each of these situations.

The complexities provoked when the law encounters thorny moral questions of this kind suggest that they are not susceptible to resolution by slogans. 'The right to die', 'autonomy', 'self-determination', and 'sanctity of life' are generously deployed in these debates, but the law must develop careful, reflective answers that best serve the public interest (see Box 9). Judges may not be the most appropriate arbiters, but is there an alternative? Two decisions of the courts (one English, one American) illustrate the perplexity involved.

The English case arose out of a crush that occurred at a football stadium in 1989 (see Chapter 2). Anthony Bland sustained hypoxic brain damage which left him in a PVS. Though his brain stem continued to function, his cerebral cortex (the seat of consciousness, communicative activity, and voluntary movement) was destroyed through lack of oxygen, but he was not 'legally

Box 9 The Dutch approach

The law in the Netherlands sets out in fairly lucid terms the conditions that must be satisfied before a doctor is permitted to end a patient's life.

Doctors involved in voluntary euthanasia or suicide must:

a. be convinced that the patient's request was voluntary, well-considered and lasting

b. be convinced that the patient's suffering was unremitting and unbearable

c. have informed the patient of the situation and prospects

d. have reached the conclusion with the patient that there was no reasonable alternative

e. have consulted at least one other physician

f. have carried out the procedure in a medically appropriate fashion.

Section 293(2) of the Dutch Criminal Code

dead'. The judge, Lord Justice Hoffmann (as he then was), described his wretched state as follows:

> He lies in … hospital … fed liquid food by a pump through a tube passing through his nose and down the back of his throat into his stomach. His bladder is emptied through a catheter inserted through his penis, which from time to time has caused infections requiring dressing and antibiotic treatment. His stiffened joints have caused his limbs to be rigidly contracted so that his arms are tightly flexed across his chest and his legs unnaturally contorted. Reflex movements in his throat cause him to vomit and dribble. Of all of this, and the presence of members of his family who take turns to visit him, Anthony Bland has no consciousness at all … The darkness and oblivion … will never depart.

There was no prospect of any improvement in Bland's condition that could endure for a substantial period. His doctors applied to the court for permission to withdraw his ventilation, antibiotics, and artificial feeding and hydration regime, while continuing otherwise to treat him so as to allow him to die with dignity and minimal pain and suffering. The official solicitor (who acts for those under a disability) argued that this would constitute a breach of the doctor's duty to his patient, and a criminal offence.

The House of Lords (the United Kingdom's court of final appeal, now the Supreme Court) regarded the right of self-determination as more important than the right to life. The doctor should respect his patient's rights in that order. This is especially compelling where the patient has, in anticipation of his succumbing to a condition such as PVS, expressed his clear wish not to be given medical care, including artificial feeding, calculated to keep him alive. But, though all five judges agreed that Bland's life should be allowed to end, there is no clear consensus in respect of precisely what the law was or should be. All recognized both the sanctity of life and the autonomy of the patient, but how were these values to be reconciled in the absence of an explicit expression of instructions by Bland? For Lord Goff, the answer lay in protecting the best interests of the patient. But what interests can an insensate patient have? Lord Goff thought they consisted partly in the anguish and stress to others. Lords Keith and Mustill were doubtful, the latter declaring:

> [I]t seems to me to be stretching the concept of personal rights beyond breaking point to say that Anthony Bland has an interest in ending these sources of others' distress. Unlike the conscious patient he does not know what is happening to his body...The distressing truth which must not be shirked is that the proposed conduct is not in the best interests of Anthony Bland, for he has no best interests of any kind.

This approach seems to echo the stance adopted by several courts in the United States and Canada. In the celebrated decision of the United States Supreme Court of *Cruzan*, for instance (involving a patient in a PVS whose parents sought to persuade the court that, though she had not expressed this in a 'living will', their daughter would not have wanted to continue living), it was held that the state had an interest in the sanctity, and hence the preservation, of life. Similarly the state's interest in preserving life looms large in the judgments.

In the event, the House of Lords ruled that the withdrawal of Bland's nutrition and hydration did not constitute a criminal offence because any hope of Bland recovering had been abandoned, and, though the termination of his life was not in his best interests, his best interests in being kept alive had also evaporated along with the justification for the non-consensual regime and the duty to maintain it. In the absence of this duty, the withdrawal of nutrition and hydration was not a criminal offence.

There have been other heart-rending cases. Most recently Debbie Purdy, a British woman suffering from primary progressive multiple sclerosis, wished to end her life which the disease had rendered unendurable, but was concerned that if her husband assisted her suicide by accompanying her to a Swiss clinic to die, he might be prosecuted for the offence of aiding or abetting her death. Under the Suicide Act 1961 this carries a maximum sentence of fourteen years' imprisonment. Her case was eventually heard by the House of Lords, which decided that the failure to clarify how the statute was applied in practice was an infringement of her right to a private and family life under the Human Rights Act. It required the Director of Public Prosecutions to formulate a clear policy specifying the facts and circumstances that will be taken into account in deciding, in a case such as Purdy's, whether or not to consent to a prosecution under the Suicide Act. Miss Purdy later died in a hospice.

Courts around the world cannot circumvent these distressing dilemmas. Their burden would be considerably eased by the existence of a 'living will' in which an individual stipulates something along the lines of the following:

> If, as a result of physical or mental incapacity, I become unable to participate in decisions concerning my medical care and treatment, and subsequently develop any of the medical conditions described below (from which two independent physicians certify I have no reasonable prospect of recovering), I declare that my life should not be sustained by artificial means.

The two problems of live and death coalesced recently in a landmark Irish case which involved a pregnant woman who had been declared clinically dead after suffering a severe head injury. It followed another case in which a woman died after seeking a termination of her pregnancy when she was told she was miscarrying; her request was refused as the foetus was alive and her life appeared not to be in danger. She died of blood poisoning days after miscarrying. The case attracted worldwide publicity, raising questions about the application of the country's strict abortion law.

In the more recent case the doctors also rejected the pregnant woman's family's appeals to turn off her life support; they feared liability for negligence or even murder. By doing so they would also end the life of the foetus. The matter came before the High Court of Ireland which, despite the fact that the Irish constitution protects the right to life, accepted the evidence of seven medical witnesses that the foetus had 'nothing but distress and death in prospect'. It would not survive even with life support. The court decided that since the mother's body was increasingly vulnerable to infection, high temperature and blood pressure, and fungus growth, which endangered the life of the unborn child, the life support machine could legally be switched off.

The court recognized that Ireland's constitutional prohibition of abortion obliges authorities to defend equally the right to life of the mother and the foetus. Where, however, the mother is already dead, the rights of the living foetus 'must prevail over the feelings of grief and respect for a mother who is no longer living'. The judges left open the possibility that similar cases might be treated differently where the foetus was much closer to birth. The case has led to calls for by pro-choice advocates and some doctors for the repeal of the constitutional provision banning abortion.

Torture

The use of torture to obtain information or as a form of punishment has a long history. From crucifixion to the rack, thumbscrew, and a variety of other inventive medieval contrivances, the cruel infliction of pain has for centuries been a key tool in the hands of inquisitors and even courts. Though the English Bill of Rights of 1689 provides that 'cruel and unusual punishment' shall not be inflicted (a provision adopted in the Eighth Amendment to the US Constitution), and is prohibited by a number of declarations: Article 3 of the European Convention on Human Rights, Article 3 of the Geneva Conventions of 1949, Article 7 of the International Covenant on Civil and Political

Rights of 1966, and the United Nations Convention Against Torture of 1984, the practice persists in many countries.

Most recently, a controversial US Senate Select Committee on Intelligence reported on the CIA's Detention and Interrogation Program and its use of various forms of torture (or 'enhanced interrogation techniques'). It revealed the extent of the CIA's interrogation and detention programmes, concluding that the agency's use of torture was both brutal and ineffective, and that the CIA repeatedly lied about its efficacy. The report's chairwoman claimed that torture 'regularly resulted in fabricated information', describing the programme as 'a stain on our values and on our history'. Former Vice-President Dick Cheney, however, said the report was 'full of crap', 'deeply flawed', and a 'terrible piece of work'. He spoke for a number of critics who denounced the document on the grounds that torture of detainees was both necessary and effective in thwarting terrorist attacks.

The so-called 'war on terror' launched in the wake of the horror of 11 September 2001, has unleashed a wave of anti-terrorist legislation in several jurisdictions that, in effect, authorizes torture. In 2006 the US enacted the Military Commissions Act which permits the executive to conduct military tribunals of 'enemy combatants' and hold them indefinitely without judicial review. Evidence gained through degrading or humiliating treatment would be admissible in the tribunals.

Aside from the precise definition of torture, its legality, or its effectiveness, is it ever morally acceptable (see Box 10)? A common scenario used to justify torture is the so-called 'ticking time bomb' hypothesis. Suppose a known terrorist has planted a nuclear bomb that is set to detonate within a few hours, but he refuses to disclose its location. Surely, it is argued, it would be morally wrong *not* to torture him in order to save the lives of thousands. Is not the torturing of a single individual justified in order to protect the many? An obvious response to this ostensibly

Box 10 Justifying torture?

[W]e should stand for a *threshold absolutism* on torture. We must insist on the wrongfulness of torture, even if we accept that there might be exceptional cases where the wrong may be excused. Consider the intuition that while we might give soldiers in a just war medals and a parade, we should recoil at doing this for torturers...Above all, we must never make such excuses *ex ante*, as a matter of open law or secret policy, much less make torture permissible in war, where it will indeed metastasize... [V]iolations of such a foundational norm must seek pardon *ex post facto*, not license *ex ante*. It may seem paradoxical that the justified may still be wrong, but such paradoxes are a feature of the tragic in the human condition, and we must mark the outer limits of hell as best we can.

Gregory Fried, 'Review of Uwe Steinhoff, *On the Ethics of Torture*'

compelling claim is its artificiality. This situation has never occurred, and is highly unlikely ever to do so.

The argument ultimately boils down to disagreement between those of a consequentialist disposition who defend torture where it is the only way to prevent a greater harm, on the one hand, and those who adopt a deontologist view (certain acts are intrinsically right or wrong regardless of their consequences) who believe that torture is always wrong, on the other. But what if the law explicitly authorizes torture? Professor Alan Dershowitz has controversially argued that in the face of extremists who threaten our security, the law ought to provide for torture to be used when it is shown to be the only method by which to avoid serious injury:

The question is not whether some torture would or would not be used in the ticking bomb case—it surely would. The dilemma is whether it would be done openly, pursuant to a previously established legal procedure, or whether it would be done secretly, in violation of existing law. This is the important policy issue about which I have tried to begin a debate: how should a democracy make difficult choice-of-evil decisions in situations for which there is no good resolution?

But the idea of 'torture warrants', even when security is threatened, sticks in the throats of civil libertarians who question whether courts of law should be asked to authorize or legitimate a practice that is widely regarded as reprehensible? Ought judges, they ask, to be drawn into questions involving the deliberate infliction of cruelty? There is something to be said for ensuring that in a democratic society the use of torture should be above the 'radar screen of accountability' rather than operate in a surreptitious manner beyond the reach of the law. But it is doubtful whether this approach will find favour with those who are expected to administer it—the judges. In the face of the rise of terrorism and the emergence of groups such as Islamic State, these questions are unlikely to go away.

Doing what comes naturally

Moral questions have, of course, engrossed philosophers since Aristotle. Theories of natural law have sought to resolve the conflict between what 'is' and what 'ought' to be. Its fundamental contention, in simple terms, is that what naturally *is, ought* to be. What occurs in nature is good; we should seek to pursue it. Reproduction is natural; therefore we ought to create offspring. As Cicero, the Roman lawyer, put it:

> True law is right reason in agreement with Nature; it is of universal application, unchanging and everlasting.... It is a sin to try to alter this law, nor is it allowable to attempt to repeal any part of it, and it is impossible to abolish it entirely.... [God] is the author of this law, its promulgator, and its enforcing judge.

Contemporary accounts of natural law owe much to the Catholic Church, especially the careful works of the Dominican, St Thomas

Aquinas (1225–74), whose principal work *Summa Theologiae* contains the most comprehensive statement of Christian doctrine on the subject. In 17th-century Europe, the exposition of compeptic divisions of the law purported to be based on natural law. Hugo Groot (1583–1645), or Grotius as he is usually called, is associated with the secularization of natural law. In his influential work *De Jure Belli ac Pacis*, he asserts that even if God did not exist, natural law would have the same content. This was a significant foundation for the emergent discipline of public international law.

The 18th century saw Sir William Blackstone (1723–80) in England proclaiming the significance of natural law in his *Commentaries on the Laws of England*. Blackstone begins his great work by espousing classical natural law doctrine—as if to consecrate English law by this appeal to God-given principles, an attitude that drew the fire of the utilitarian philosopher and legal and social reformer Jeremy Bentham (1748–1832), who derided natural law as 'a mere work of the fancy'.

Despite his scorn, natural law has been exploited to justify revolutions—notably the American and the French—on the ground that the law infringed individuals' *natural* rights. The American Revolution against British colonial rule was founded on an appeal to the natural rights of all Americans, in the lofty words of the Declaration of Independence of 1776, to 'life, liberty and the pursuit of happiness'. As the Declaration puts it, 'We hold these truths to be self-evident, that all men are created equal, that they are endowed by their Creator with certain unalienable rights.' Equally rousing sentiments were included in the French Déclaration des Droits de l'Homme et du Citoyen of 26 August 1789, which refers to the 'natural rights' of mankind.

And natural law theory implicitly underpinned the Nuremberg war trials of Nazi officials, which established the principle that certain acts constituted 'crimes against humanity' even if at the time they were committed they did not violate particular

provisions of the positive law. The judges in these trials did not appeal explicitly to natural law theory, but their judgments exemplify an acknowledgement of the idea that the law is not the exclusive measure of right and wrong.

Our epoch is one of growing public accountability. Or, more precisely, we now seek to indict the perpetrators of genocide and other crimes against humanity, and the impunity enjoyed by malevolent government officials, their collaborators, and military commanders is gradually being eroded. The recent establishment of the International Criminal Court at The Hague is a remarkable recognition that evil dictators and their henchmen should not be allowed go scot-free. Although the current United States administration has set its face against the court (principally because of fears both that it would undermine US sovereignty over judicial matters relating to American subjects and because its troops might face prosecution), this could change in the future. The court's jurisdiction is confined to 'the most serious crimes of concern to the international community as a whole'. This includes crimes against humanity, genocide, war crimes, and crimes of aggression.

At the time of writing the court has nine cases under investigation, all in Africa. It has charged thirty-six individuals and issued arrest warrants for another twenty-eight. Proceedings against twenty-five are currently proceeding.

Human rights

No serious analysis of law and morals can be conducted without reference to the concept of human rights. Ever since 1215 when Magna Carta proclaimed the importance of individual liberty, the legal systems of democratic societies subscribe, to a greater or lesser extent, to the rule of law (discussed in Chapter 1) which embodies the notion of individual rights. Nowadays moral claims are frequently transformed into moral rights: individuals assert

their rights to a whole range of goods, including life, work, health, education, and housing. Peoples assert their right to self-determination, sovereignty, and free trade.

In the legal context, rights have acquired significance so profound that they are sometimes regarded as synonymous with law itself. Declarations of political rights are often perceived as the trademark of contemporary democratic statehood. And the inevitable clash between rival rights is among the distinctive features of a liberal society.

On the international front, a panoply of human rights conventions and declarations attest to the strength of rights talk. The United Nations Universal Declaration of Human Rights of 1948, and the International Covenants on Civil and Political Rights, and on Economic, Social and Cultural Rights in 1976, reveal, at least in theory, a dedication by the international community to the universal conception and protection of human rights. It demonstrates a remarkable degree of cross-cultural accord among nations.

In a world increasingly threatened by terrorism, there is a delicate conflict between freedom and security, a subject upon which I reflect in Chapter 6.

Chapter 4
Courts

Courts personify the law. In the more grandiloquent accounts of law and the legal system, judges are its custodians, guardians of its values: sentinels of justice and fair play. Yet we do think of judges as embodying fairness, evenhandedness, and impartiality. And an independent judiciary is an important hallmark of the rule of law. The jurist, Ronald Dworkin, memorably observed that 'courts are the capitals of law's empire, and judges are its princes'.

Judges are not, however, always perceived in these lofty terms. In the words of a distinguished English judge:

> [T]he public entertain a range of views, not all consistent (one minute they are senile and out of touch, the next the very people to conduct a detailed and searching inquiry; one minute port-gorged dinosaurs imposing savage sentences on hapless miscreants, the next wishy-washy liberals unwilling to punish anyone properly for anything), although often unfavourable.

It is especially the judges' role in criminal trials that excites public interest. The drama of the law court is irresistible to novelists and playwrights, as well as film and television scriptwriters. In the English-speaking world, several come instantly to mind. Dickens's *Bleak House* is a wonderful example. Albert Camus's *The Fall*, Kafka's *The Trial*, and the popular portrayal of the judicial process in Harper Lee's *To Kill a Mockingbird*, Scott Turow's *Presumed Innocent*, John Mortimer's *Rumpole of the Bailey* series, and bestseller John Grisham's novels are other striking examples. Shakespeare provides an unforgettable representation of the idea of justice and the forensic process in *The Merchant of Venice*. Courtroom dramas on film abound: *Judgment at Nuremberg, Witness for the Prosecution*, and *Anatomy of a Murder* are outstanding examples. Courts and lawyers are also the stuff of many a successful television series, though their depiction is often based less on reality than drama. *The Good Wife, Ally McBeal, The Practice*, and *LA Law* are recent instances.

It is easy to see why court proceedings fascinate and entertain. The theatre of a criminal trial can be gripping. The clash of lawyers, the uncertain fate of the accused, the lurid evidence—excite a voyeuristic curiosity and genuine interest. And occasionally the fictional representation of the judicial process is no less spectacular than authentic trials which, particularly in the United States, are often televised live. Where a celebrity is on trial, cameras in court guarantee an enormous audience of viewers—the more gruesome the alleged crime, the better. The trials of celebrities such as O. J. Simpson, Oscar Pistorius, and Phil Spector attracted millions of viewers globally. Few trials, however, achieve this level of vivacity or glamour; they tend to be dull and tedious.

While a criminal trial may be enlivened by engaging evidence, civil trials normally lack this piquancy. The court is here engaged in the resolution of a dispute. The lawyers who represent the parties seek to persuade the court of the merits of their case. In a common law trial one side cites a previous judgment, arguing that the present case is sufficiently similar to the earlier one that it ought to be followed. The other side seeks to distinguish this precedent by identifying its often subtle differences. This is the essence of legal reasoning. Should the losing party appeal, the arguments will be rehearsed before more senior judges.

Judges unquestionably exercise onerous responsibilities:

> It is an awesome thing to go forward before the judge and await the
> utterances of his decision ... He symbolizes the merger of conceptual
> justice with organized coercion, the rational human with the mass
> brute. In him have been remitted the ideals of his culture and the
> power to compel submission. When a citizen stands in court he
> feels the immediate impact of that power; it is all assembled and
> concentrated there on him.

The role of judges is fundamental to the common law; the pivotal
force of the judicial function drives the legal system both in theory
and in practice. And though it may be less significant in the
codified systems of Continental Europe, the influence of judges
cannot be overstated.

The judge is thus the archetypal legal institution. In his robed and
exalted independence, he represents the very apotheosis of justice.
The 'social service' that he renders to the community is, in the words
of the English judge Lord Devlin, 'the removal of a sense of injustice'.
The neutrality that informs his judgments in the settlement of
disputes is nothing short of an article of faith in a free and just
society. The dispassionate judge is the quintessence of a democratic
system of government. And the ostensible delineation between
legislation and adjudication is among its most celebrated hallmarks.

Although this attractive and enduring perception of the judicial
function is regarded by cynics as a myth, no amount of scepticism
can easily dislodge the image of the judge as keeper of the law,
protector and repository of justice (see Box 11). Nor is this to deny
that judges are, like all of us, tainted by personal predilections
and political prejudices. Yet occasionally it is contended that to
acknowledge judicial frailty is, in some sense, subversive, 'as if
judges', as the illustrious American judge Benjamin Cardozo put
it, 'must lose respect and confidence by the reminder that they are
subject to human limitations'.

Box 11 The judges' moral responsibility

A judge must decide not just who shall have what, but who has behaved well, who has met the responsibilities of citizenship, and who by design or greed or insensitivity has ignored his own responsibilities or exaggerated theirs to him. If this judgment is unfair, then the community has inflicted a moral injury on one of its members because it has stamped him in some degree or dimension an outlaw. The injury is gravest when an innocent person is convicted of a crime, but it is substantial enough when a plaintiff with a sound claim is turned away from court or a defendant leaves with an undeserved stigma.

Ronald Dworkin, *Law's Empire*

Courts play a central role in every legal system. But what precisely is that role? What of the political function of judges? What of their appointment, election, and accountability? Is the jury system a valuable element in the administration of criminal justice, especially in complex commercial criminal trials? Is the adversarial system of common law countries superior to the inquisitorial system of civil law jurisdictions? Are courts the best forum for resolving disputes? Can judges be genuinely impartial or objective? What is the purpose of a criminal trial? Are certain courts—such as the United States Supreme Court—too political? Should judges be elected? Is the jury system effective and fair? This chapter will attempt to answer some of these questions.

What do judges do?

In seeking to unravel the mysteries of how judges decide cases, we are engaged in a quest for the meaning of law itself: a theory of what constitutes law is, of necessity, presupposed in the act of judging, as well as any account of it. The orthodox, so-called 'legal positivist' model perceives law as a system of rules; where there is no applicable rule or there is a degree of ambiguity or uncertainty, the judge has a discretion to fill in the gaps in the law. This view is most closely associated with Professor H. L. A. Hart. Legal positivists such as him generally describe law by reference to formal rather than moral criteria. In their pursuit of a 'scientific' approach to law and legal rules, they argue that the law as laid down (*positum*) should be kept separate—for the purpose of study and analysis—from the law as it *ought* morally to be. In other words, that a clear distinction must be drawn between 'ought' (that which is morally desirable) and 'is' (that which actually exists). Positivists do share the view that the most effective method of *analysing* and *understanding* law and the legal system involves suspending moral judgment until it is established what it is we are seeking to explain.

This view has been challenged most forcefully by Professor Dworkin, who denies that law consists exclusively of rules. In addition to rules (which 'are applicable in an all-or-nothing fashion'), there are non-rule standards: 'principles' and 'policies' which, unlike rules, have 'the dimension of weight or importance'. A 'principle' is 'a standard that is to be observed, not because it will advance or secure an economic, political, or social situation..., but because it is a requirement of justice or fairness or some other dimension of morality'. A 'policy', on the other hand, is 'that kind of standard that sets out a goal to be reached, generally an improvement in some economic, political, or social feature of the community'.

When the judge can find no immediately applicable rule, or where no settled rule dictates a decision, the judge is called upon to weigh competing principles, which are no less part of the law for their not being rules. In such 'hard cases', since a judge is not expected to resort to his personal preference in arriving at a decision, he has, contrary to the positivist view, no real discretion. There is always one right answer, and it is the judge's task to find it (in 'hard cases') by weighing competing principles and determining the rights of the parties in the case before him.

This model of adjudication has an obvious appeal to democratic theory: judges do not legislate; they merely enforce those rights that have in the main already been enacted by a representative legislature. Indeed, Dworkin's thesis springs from a concern to 'define and defend a liberal theory of law' and, in contradistinction to the positivists, to 'take rights seriously'. It is principally an argument from democracy; Dworkin's concern to eliminate strong judicial discretion is premised on the offensiveness of judges, who are generally unelected officials unanswerable to the electorate, wielding legislative or quasi-legislative power.

What is a court?

The ubiquity of conflict among humans necessitates some forum in which disputes might be fairly resolved (see Box 12). Courts of some kind are a prerequisite of all legal systems. They have power, authority—or what lawyers called 'jurisdiction'—over specified criminal, civil, and other matters. This entails that their decisions (which are ultimately supported by force) are accepted as authoritative by the parties—who would be unlikely to do so if they did not trust in the independence and impartiality of the professional judges on the bench.

Courts err. Judges are not exempt from human frailty, and there is thus a need for their mistakes to be rectified. The

---

Box 12 Right to a fair hearing

All persons shall be equal before the courts and tribunals. In the determination of any criminal charge against him, or of his rights and obligations in a suit at law, everyone shall be entitled to a fair and public hearing by a competent, independent and impartial tribunal established by law.

Article 14(1) International Covenant on Civil and Political Rights obvious injustice of a wrongly convicted defendant is assuaged by granting him the right of appeal. Equally, the losing party in a civil case may have legitimate legal grounds upon which to argue that the trial court was mistaken in its interpretation of the law. Appealing to a higher court requires a hierarchy that distinguishes between courts 'of first instance' and appellate courts. Some trial courts operate with a judge and a jury: juries are responsible for making findings of fact under the direction of the judge, who decides the law. This combination constitutes the judgment of the court. In other trial courts, both fact and law are decided by the judge.

Appellate courts in common law jurisdictions review the decisions of trial courts or of lower appellate courts. Their task is generally restricted to considering questions of law: did the trial court, for example, apply and interpret the law correctly? Normally they do not hear evidence of factual issues, though should new evidence have emerged, an appeal court may evaluate it in order to determine whether the case should be remitted to a court of first instance to be retried.

Courts everywhere naturally follow procedures which, in some countries, have grown bulky and Byzantine. In criminal trials, these procedures are broadly differentiated on the basis of the role of the judge. The common law adopts an 'adversarial' system, while civil law countries adopt an 'inquisitorial' (or 'accusatorial') system. While this distinction is frequently exaggerated, the two approaches do differ in a fairly fundamental way. The common law judge acts as a disinterested umpire who rarely descends into the dust of the fray. Civil law judges, on the other hand, play a more active role in the trial.

The Continental *juge d'instruction* is directly involved in the decision whether to prosecute. The office originated in France, and exists in a number of other European countries, including Spain, Greece, Switzerland, the Netherlands, Belgium, and

Portugal. They are often portrayed as a cross between a prosecutor and a judge, but this is not strictly accurate, for they do not decide whether to lay a charge; that is a matter for the public prosecutor, from whose office they are completely independent. Their principal duty is, as the title implies, to investigate the evidence both for and against the suspect, who they have the power to interrogate. They will also question victims and witnesses. They may visit the crime scene and attend any post-mortem. In the course of his investigation, they may authorize detention, grant bail, and order searches and seizures of evidence.

It is important to note that their job is not to determine the merits of the case, but to examine the evidence in order to decide whether the suspect should be charged. If they rule in the affirmative, the case is transmitted to a trial court with which they have no connection, and which is not bound to follow their decision. Their function is thus not wholly unlike common law committal proceedings or the American grand jury, both of which are designed to screen the evidence to establish whether it crosses the threshold of chargeability. Though supervised by a judge, a grand jury is presided over by a prosecutor. It has the power to subpoena witnesses in pursuit of evidence against the suspect.

Both major systems have their virtues and shortcomings. It is generally asserted—particularly by common lawyers—that the common law attaches greater significance and value to the presumption of innocence by placing a heavier burden on the prosecution to prove its case 'beyond reasonable doubt'. This is doubtful. A defendant in an Italian or French court is afforded essentially the same rights and protections as one in Florida. All democratic states recognize the presumption of innocence; indeed, it is a requirement of Article 6 of the European Convention on Human Rights which applies to the forty-seven Council of Europe member states.

Criticism of the adversarial system is not confined to civil lawyers. The occasionally grotesque conduct of criminal trials, especially in America, is an embarrassment to common lawyers. The process sometimes descends into burlesque in which the attorneys abuse the adversarial process and appear to lose sight of the purpose of the institution. This is mainly evident in high-profile, televised celebrity trials with overpaid lawyers histrionically playing to the cameras and the jury. Many civil lawyers are also astonished by the way in which the common law criminal justice system appears to benefit affluent defendants who are able to afford large legal teams. The trials of O. J. Simpson and Michael Jackson are only the most conspicuous recent examples.

Common law prosecutions are generally pursued by way of a charge or indictment against the defendant in the name of the government, the state, or, in Britain, the Crown. This normally follows a preliminary hearing of some kind to determine whether the prosecution evidence is adequate. To discharge its burden of proof, the prosecution will call witnesses and present its evidence against the defendant. The defence may then argue that there is 'no case to answer'. If this fails (as it normally does), witnesses and evidence are presented by the defence. Witnesses are cross-examined by the opposing counsel, but the defendant has the 'right of silence': he or she need say nothing in their defence, but should they decide to give evidence, the defendant is required to submit to cross-examination. In the United States this right is protected by the Fifth Amendment to the constitution. Both sides then present their closing arguments. Where there is a jury, the judge gives them their instructions. Its members then deliberate in private. Some jurisdictions require the jury to return a unanimous verdict, in others a majority suffices.

Sentence

If convicted, the defendant is sentenced. This normally occurs after the court is apprised of her previous criminal record, if she has one, as well as other information about her character. Where she faces the prospect of a custodial sentence, reports may be submitted to the court concerning the defendant's background: education, family, employment history, and so on. Psychological or medical reports may also be presented, along with evidence, including witnesses to testify to her unimpeachable integrity. This may be followed by a moving plea in mitigation of sentence in which his lawyer attempts to convince the court that the accused is a victim of the cruel vicissitudes and privations of life: poverty, manipulation by others, poor parenting, and other equally powerful forces that were beyond her control and are where the true responsibility for her crime lies.

Every legal system will, of course, have a different range of sentences available to a trial court. These may include imprisonment, a fine, a probation order, a community service order, or a suspended sentence of imprisonment (the term of imprisonment is suspended for, say, two years; if he commits an offence during this period, it may trigger the original sentence).

It is always open to the convicted defendant to appeal to a higher court, which does not hear the case again, but peruses the record of the proceedings in search of any mistakes that could justify a retrial. In certain circumstances, the prosecution may appeal a sentence that it considers too lenient.

Civil trials

The disparity between the common and civil law approaches is less marked in civil trials. French law, however, has come close to eliminating civil trials: the extensive pre-trial preparation undertaken by the *juge de la mise en état* results in the pleadings and evidence being reduced to writing. The lawyers merely present brief summaries of what the court already has before it. Moreover, the standard of proof in French civil trials is no lower in civil cases than it is in criminal trials.

In civil law countries 'ordinary' judges preside over 'ordinary' courts. Their jurisdiction, broadly speaking, involves the application of the civil, commercial, and penal codes, and the legislation that complements the codes. In France, the highest court in the ordinary court structure is the Cour de Cassation (Supreme Court of Cassation) which comprises eighty-five trial judges (*conseillers*) and some forty deputy judges who sit in six rotating specialized panels (five civil and one criminal) and, in certain circumstances, in combined panels or plenary sessions. It has discretion to review only questions of statutory interpretation. Germany has a number of independent judicial systems, each with its own supreme court. Most civilian systems also incorporate a group of administrative courts with separate jurisdiction.

Common law systems adopt an adversarial procedure in civil trials as well. Instead of the government or Crown proceeding against the defendant, an aggrieved plaintiff (or 'claimant') sues the defendant, usually for damages, i.e. monetary compensation (for a tort, breach of contract, or other civil wrong). Both sides are free to call witnesses, and the rules of evidence are broadly the same as in criminal trials. An important difference, however, is that whereas, as we saw, the burden of proof in a criminal trial is 'beyond reasonable doubt', the plaintiff in a civil case need only prove his case 'on a balance of probabilities'.

Who are the judges?

Common law judges are, with the conspicuous exception of the United States, appointed from the ranks of senior lawyers, while European Continental judges are recruited in the style of the civil service. They are generally employed directly from university through some form of public examination with no requirement of previous professional experience. Successful candidates are appointed at the bottom of the career ladder; professional training occurs within the judiciary, with promotions depending on merit. Public competition is considered the most effective method of maintaining the professional standing and the independence of the judiciary. It checks political partiality and nepotism, but the fear of prejudicing promotion may inhibit a true spirit of independence from the executive branch. There is also the likelihood that since private practice is normally significantly more lucrative than a career on the bench, the more gifted law graduate may be discouraged from entering the service.

The position in the United States is complex. The federal courts are divided into three tiers: the Supreme Court, the Circuit Court of Appeals, and the District Court. Under the US Constitution, the president has the power to nominate and, in conjunction with the senate, appoint judges of all three courts. He nominates candidates to the senate after receiving recommendations from the Department of Justice and White House staff. The Department of Justice screens prospective nominees, followed by an investigation of the candidate by the FBI. Views are sought on the nominee's suitability from the American Bar Association.

The White House Counsel's Office also plays a role; it works together with the Department of Justice and members of the senate, and considers recommendations by members of the House of Representatives, state governors, bar associations, and other bodies. The Senate Judiciary Committee scrutinizes the credentials of candidates. Should it reject a nomination, it is returned to the president to produce another name. Nominations by the Senate Judiciary Committee are considered by the senate in executive sessions. Non-controversial candidates tend to be unanimously confirmed. When a contentious nomination is made, however, a debate ensues. An adverse recommendation by the Senate Judiciary Committee inexorably results in rejection of the candidate by the senate. Of the 151 potential judges nominated so far, only twelve have been formally rejected by the senate. A successful nominee is formally appointed by the president.

The protracted nature of the process, including filibustering by senators, as well as the predictable ideological dimension of the system, has attracted considerable criticism. Its detractors contend that it undermines the independence of the judiciary. Defenders of the method, however, claim that the president and senate exercise a vital and legitimate check on the composition and standing of the federal judiciary.

At the non-federal level, judges are elected in twenty American states; this is a rarity, not encountered in any other common or civil law jurisdiction. Although it may appeal to the democrat, it unavoidably transforms judges into politicians who, to keep their jobs, must appeal to popular sentiments and prejudices. While it may be true that an elective system is preferable to one of nomination under a corrupt government which appoints compliant judges regardless of their ability, few lawyers support what John Stuart Mill called 'one of the most dangerous errors ever yet committed by democracy'.

Dissatisfaction with the method of judicial appointment, based largely on the unrepresentative nature of appointees (few women or members of racial minorities), has led to the adoption of judicial appointments commissions which seek to bring greater transparency and fairness to the process (see Figure 7). The commissions are charged with responsibility for selection. They exist in some states of the United States, as well as in Canada, Scotland, South Africa, Israel, Ireland, and in a number of other European countries, including England and Wales, where since 2006 it functions as an independent non-departmental public body. Applicants for judicial office are required to submit a nine-page application form; short-listed candidates are interviewed. They are evaluated according to five criteria: intellectual capacity; personal qualities (integrity, independence, judgment, decisiveness, objectivity, ability, willingness to learn); ability to understand and deal fairly; authority and communication skills; and efficiency.

7. **Members of the Supreme Court of Canada, four of whom are women, including the Chief Justice.**

The politics of the judiciary

Though the US Constitution nowhere explicitly confers on the Supreme Court the power of judicial review, it has, since the seminal case of *Marbury v Madison* in 1803, asserted the right to strike down laws that it regards as in conflict with the provisions of the Constitution. This, the most muscular form of judicial review, entails a court of appointed judges (albeit with senate approval) exercising control over democratically enacted laws. In doing so, the court has effected major social and political transformations by declaring as unconstitutional a wide range of legislation by states on matters as diverse as abortion, contraception, racial and sexual discrimination, and freedom of religion, speech, and assembly.

In the United Kingdom, the court of final appeal is the Supreme Court, which in 2009 replaced the Judicial Committee of the House of Lords. Its principal function is to hear appeals from the UK's three legal systems: England and Wales, Northern Ireland, and Scotland. Despite its name it lacks the power of the Supreme Court of the United States to overturn legislation enacted by parliament. It may, however, declare legislation to be incompatible with the rights specified in the European Convention on Human Rights, and it can set aside secondary legislation which, for example, it finds to be *ultra vires* (beyond the powers) of the body purporting to pass it.

The Supreme Court of India has, with broad public support, exhibited a high degree of judicial activism in a number of areas of social, political, and economic life, including marriage, the environment, human rights, agrarian reforms, and the law governing elections. The judges have frequently described the constitution as more than a political document; it is considered an abiding declaration of 'social philosophy'. And this philosophy is steeped in egalitarian values that represent a commitment to reform society to correspond to the principles of social justice that inspired the framers of the constitution.

One striking feature of the court's jurisprudence is the concept of public interest litigation, whereby the poor obtain access to the courts. The court has held that legal redress for the deprived should not be encumbered by the restrictions of the adversarial system. Similarly, it has accorded a liberal interpretation of Article 21 of the constitution which provides that 'No person shall be deprived of his life or personal liberty except according to procedure established by law.' This has engendered a considerable expansion in substantive individual rights.

Under its post-apartheid constitution, the South African Constitutional Court has the power to interpret the constitution and has handed down far-reaching decisions, including declaring capital punishment to be unlawful and upholding the right to housing, the state's constitutional duty to provide effective remedies against domestic violence, and the right to equality.

Weaker forms of judicial review exist which permit the legislature and executive to reject the court's rulings, provided they do so publicly. They are increasingly incorporated in constitutions and legislation. So the Canadian Supreme Court has a role in constitutional interpretation, but without its judgments having an authoritative status. Should the legislature dissent from the court's interpretation it is free to re-enact the impugned legislation. Section 33 of the Canadian Charter of Rights permits the legislature to decide that a statute should survive notwithstanding its possible conflict with specified provisions of the Charter.

The New Zealand Bill of Rights of 1990 directs the courts to interpret all legislation in order to render it compatible with the Bill of Rights, but grants the courts no power to refuse to enforce statutes that are inconsistent with the Bill of Rights. Similarly, the UK's Human Rights Act of 1998 combines the interpretive directive with a judicial power to declare a statute inconsistent with guaranteed rights and a ministerial power to amend the statute speedily to comply with those rights.

Critics of strong judicial review consider objectionable the power of judges over democratically elected legislators. But even if legislative bodies were genuinely representative, the arguments in support of their being in a stronger position than courts to protect and preserve our rights are, at best, uncertain. Not only are the vicissitudes of government and party politics notoriously susceptible to sectional interest and compromise, to say nothing of corruption, but it is precisely because non-elected judges are not 'accountable' in this manner that they are often superior guardians of liberty. Moreover, the judicial temperament, training, and experience, and the forensic forum in which rights-based arguments are tested and contested, tend to tip the scales towards their adjudicative, rather than legislative, resolution. Indeed, it is hard to see how the latter would operate in practice. Since the rights in question are, by definition, in dispute, what role could elected parliamentarians play?

Sadly, one's trust in lawmakers is not often vindicated. Though sometimes contentious, certain fundamental rights are best kept off-limits to legislators, or at least beyond the reach of normal party political machinations. Would the civil liberties of African Americans have been recognized sooner without the Supreme Court's historic *Brown v Board of Education* decision in 1954, which held that separate educational facilities for black and white pupils was 'inherently unequal'? (See Chapter 6.)

Is the South African Constitutional Court not more likely to defend human rights than its new, democratic parliament? Have the judgments of the European Court of Human Rights (which, sitting in Strasbourg, considers complaints concerning alleged violations of the European Convention for the Protection of Human Rights and Fundamental Freedoms committed by States Parties) not enhanced civil liberties in, say, Britain? The court has ruled against the British government on frequent occasions, requiring it to amend its domestic law on a variety of Convention-protected rights, including the right of privacy, the right against the use of corporal punishment, and the rights of mental health patients.

Trial by jury

In common law systems the notion of being tried by a jury of 'one's peers' is frequently regarded as an article of faith. Its importance is reflected in the words of the judge, Lord Devlin, who in 1956 wrote: 'Trial by jury is more than an instrument of justice and more than a wheel of the constitution; it is the lamp that shows that freedom lives.'

Jurisdictions differ in respect of the use of juries. Some restrict them to criminal, and not civil, trials (e.g. France where the judges sit together with the jury, who are also involved in determining the sentence to be imposed); others prescribe juries for trials of serious crimes (e.g. Canada); while in some countries

8. Oscar Pistorius on trial for killing his girlfriend.

(e.g. England and Wales) they are used in criminal cases and limited to a few specific civil cases (e.g. fraud).

South Africa abolished juries in 1969 largely on the ground that since they comprised only white persons, they were intrinsically prejudicial to 'non-white' defendants. Many who watched the homicide trial of the athlete Oscar Pistorius on television expressed surprise at the absence of a jury. Instead, in criminal trials, the judge is assisted on questions of fact by two lay 'assessors' (see Figure 8).

Most conspicuous are the jury trials in the United States, where juries are available for both civil and criminal proceedings. More than 60 per cent of jury trials are criminal trials, the rest are civil and other trials such as family court proceedings.

Among the much-vaunted virtues of the jury trial is the extent to which it operates as a curb on the power and influence of the judge. By involving (usually twelve) ordinary citizens in the administration of justice, it is argued, the values of the community may be expressed. A group of randomly selected laypersons, it is claimed, is a more democratic arbiter of guilt than a judge, who is perceived, rightly or wrongly, as an agent of the government.

Champions of the jury system also claim that fact finding is a matter of common sense that requires no legal training. And they often defend the jury's unaccountability on the ground that it fosters greater independence. It is also asserted that by acquitting a defendant against the weight of the evidence a jury can express its criticism of a bad or unpopular law.

Critics of the jury, on the other hand, generally express unease about the fact that juries, unlike judges, are not required to give reasons for their decision—made in secret—thereby opening the door to emotion and prejudice. Doubt is also voiced in respect of the ability of the average juror to comprehend complex scientific or other technical evidence. Complex commercial fraud trials, for example, generate an enormous quantity of highly specialized information. This has led to controversial proposals in Britain and elsewhere to abolish juries in these sorts of trials. Recently an exasperated judge in England dismissed a jury that had put a number of questions to him that demonstrated a 'fundamental deficit in understanding' of its role.

In addition it is sometimes thought that a jury is susceptible to domination by one or two of its more opinionated or tenacious members. The film *12 Angry Men* illustrates dramatically how juries can be swayed by a single individual's persistence. There is evidence that juries tend to acquit more often than judges or magistrates. Some suggest that this weakness may spring from jurors' perverse sympathy with the defendant.

Alternative dispute resolution (ADR)

Dissatisfaction with court-centred resolution of disputes has long been sounded by critics who regard it as, among other things, expensive, lengthy, complex, rigid, and excessively formal. ADR is increasingly available in a number of countries where, in some cases, courts actually require the parties to attempt mediation before they allow the matter to be tried. There is little doubt that, in addition to the previously mentioned drawbacks of litigation, it also lacks the confidentiality and opportunity to select the arbiter of a dispute.

There are three principal forms of ADR: mediation (in which a mediator proposes a solution without imposing it on the parties), arbitration (where parties submit their dispute to a third party who imposes a resolution upon them), and negotiation (which is voluntary without a third party to resolve the dispute).

Several university law and business schools, particularly in the United States, offer programmes on dispute and conflict resolution. Though there are a number of problems to be overcome (including, for example, poor standards and training of and funding for mediators, inadequate regulation, and limited transparency as to performance and ethics), ADR would seem to have a promising future. In the words of one of its leading protagonists:

> [M]ediation has (on our best days) some of the transcendence of religious experience but without having to go to services. This is mostly uncharted territory for ADR practitioners today, but I predict that in thirty years, it will no longer be considered strange to think of mediators as serving some of the needs that village elders served in days long ago.

Tomorrow's courts

In the future, though it is unlikely that judges will be replaced by computers, the administration of justice in many advanced societies has already undergone significant changes and will continue to do so. The courts of several jurisdictions already benefit from access to legal materials that previously would have consumed long hours of research. Virtual law libraries with sophisticated search facilities enable judges, lawyers, legal academics, and ordinary members of society to obtain rapid access to statutes, cases, and other sources of law. This will be especially helpful to less affluent countries with limited legal resources. Increasingly, judgments of the courts are posted on the Internet almost immediately after they have been handed down. There are already several excellent online legal databases such as findlaw. com and austlii.edu.au.

The electronic transcription of court proceedings, the management of cases, and the standardization of electronic documents will continue to enhance the judicial process, streamlining and reducing notorious delays. The sight of a judge laboriously taking written notes is already disappearing, but voice-recognition technology will obviate the need for note taking of any kind. Both evidence and legal sources can effortlessly be retrieved electronically. A more radical development might be the establishment of virtual courts in which the parties conduct proceedings without the need for corporeal proximity, thereby decreasing cost and delay.

Many of these advances (and there will be others) are likely to generate significant advantages for the ordinary individual seeking access to justice. Once legal information and services become more widely available, it ought to follow that the grandiose ambitions of the law and legal system will be more effectively realized.

The parties submit their dispute to one or more arbitrators by whose decision (called an 'award') they agree to be bound. Among the perceived advantages of ADR are its speed, lower cost, flexibility, and the provision of specialist arbitrators in disputes of a highly technical nature. But delays are not infrequent, and the cost may be enhanced by the requirement that the parties pay for the arbitrators. In some jurisdictions the enforcement of arbitral awards is, to say the least, challenging.

Chapter 5
Lawyers

Lawyers are an essential—if unloved—feature of every developed legal system. They are vilified, mocked, and disparaged. The humour of a multitude of lawyer jokes springs from their assault on lawyers' venality, dishonesty, and insensitivity. One jibe asks: 'How can you tell when a lawyer is lying?' The answer: 'His lips are moving'. Another sardonically laments: 'Isn't it a shame how 99 per cent of lawyers give the whole profession a bad name?' And Mark Twain is reputed to have quipped: 'It is interesting to note that criminals have multiplied of late, and lawyers have also; but I repeat myself.'

It seems futile to attempt to explain this antipathy which rests on a combination of legitimate discontent with and misunderstanding of the legal profession. It is certainly true that, along with bankers, politicians, and estate agents, lawyers attract little affection. An independent bar is, however, a vital component of the rule of law; without accessible lawyers to provide citizens with competent representation, the ideals of the legal system ring hollow. And this is acknowledged in most jurisdictions by the provision of legal aid in criminal cases. So, for example, legal aid is a right recognized by Article 6 of the European Convention on Human Rights. It requires that defendants be provided with counsel and, if they are unable to afford their own lawyer, one is made available without charge.

9. Lawyer Atticus Finch, played by Gregory Peck in the film of *To Kill a Mockingbird*.

Hollywood's heroic depiction of the lawyer, replicated in endless television series, robustly and eloquently pursuing the cause of justice for their client, is a far cry from the reality of real lawyers' lives (see Figure 9). Advocacy in court represents a small, though important, part of the profession's work. Most lawyers, however, are preoccupied daily with drafting (contracts, trusts, wills, and other documents), advising clients, conducting negotiations, conveying property, and other rather less glamorous tasks. Yet even if the majority of lawyers never set foot in a court, the essence of lawyering is the battle waged on behalf of the client. In this campaign the skills of advocacy, whether in oral or written form, are paramount. Law is often war, and the lawyer is the warrior (see Box 13).

Common lawyers

To many, the English legal profession, adaptations of which exist in common law jurisdictions of the former British Commonwealth, appears bizarre—grotesquely anachronistic with its wigs, gowns,

Box 13 Waltzing lawyers

The lawyers have twisted it into such a state of bedevilment that the original merits of the case have long disappeared from the face of the earth. It's about a Will, and the trusts under a Will—or it was, once. It's about nothing but Costs, now. We are always appearing, and disappearing, and swearing, and Interrogating, and filing, and cross-filing, and arguing, and sealing, and motioning, and referring, and reporting, and revolving about the Lord Chancellor and all his satellites, and equitably waltzing ourselves off to dusty death, about Costs. That's the great question. All the rest, by some extraordinary means, has melted away.

Charles Dickens, *Bleak House*

and stilted forms of address (see Figure 10). Though some of these quaint, archaic features have been eradicated in a few common law countries, they have shown a remarkable tenacity, especially in England. Polls of practitioners and public have proved inconclusive. Wigs on the heads of many barristers and judges seem firmly fixed for some time yet.

The origins of the common law profession are, of course, steeped in English history—and logic is thus not necessarily among its justifications. It is divided between two principal species of lawyer: barristers and solicitors. Barristers (often called 'counsel') constitute a small minority of the legal profession (roughly 10 per cent in most jurisdictions) and, rightly or wrongly, are regarded, especially by themselves, as the superior branch of the profession. Recent years have witnessed a number of fairly sweeping changes, many of which have diminished the privileges of barristers (or 'the bar'). These reforms have largely been animated by political unease regarding the soaring costs of legal services as a result of the restrictive practices of the bar.

10. **Hong Kong senior counsel in her ceremonial wig and silk gown.**

Barristers have minimal direct contact with their 'lay clients'. They are 'briefed' by solicitors, and it is normally a requirement that during meetings (or 'conferences') with clients the solicitor must be present. An exception is, however, made for certain professions, including accountants and surveyors, who may confer with a barrister without the presence of a solicitor. In most cases, however, dealings must be carried out through the solicitor who is responsible for paying the barrister's fees.

English barristers are 'called' to the bar by one of the four Inns of Court, ancient institutions that since the 16th century have governed entry to this branch of the profession. Unlike the overwhelming majority of solicitors, barristers have full rights of audience, allowing them to appear before any court. Generally, solicitors have rights of audience only before the lower courts, though in recent years the position has changed and some solicitors, certified as 'solicitor advocates', may represent their clients as advocates in the higher courts. The traditional separation is gradually breaking down.

Nevertheless, two major distinctions between the two categories of lawyer remain. First, barristers are invariably instructed by solicitors, rather than directly by the client, whereas clients go directly to solicitors. Second, unlike solicitors, barristers operate as sole practitioners, and are prohibited from forming partnerships. Instead, barristers generally form sets of chambers in which resources and expenses are shared. But it is now possible for barristers to be employed by firms of solicitors, companies, or other institutions as in-house lawyers.

Other transformations have occurred. For example, barristers are now permitted to advertise their services and their fees—a hitherto unthinkable commercial contamination. Nor are they limited to practising from a set of chambers; after three years' 'call', they may work from home.

The split profession has been attacked from a number of quarters. Why, it is not unreasonably asked, should a client effectively pay for two lawyers when, as in the United States, for instance, one will do? The case for fusion between the two branches—either formal or in effect (as exists in the common law provinces of Canada, most Australian states, New Zealand, Malaysia, and Singapore) has been met by a number of responses. In particular, it is argued by defenders of the status quo that an independent barrister offers a detached, expert evaluation of the client's case. Also, solicitors, especially those from small firms, who often lack a high degree of specialization, may draw on the expertise of a wide range of barristerial skills. This enables them to compete with larger firms who boast numerous specialists.

The United States draws no distinction: all are attorneys. Anyone who passes the state bar examination may appear in the courts of that state. Some state appeal courts require attorneys to have a certificate of admission to plead and practise in that court. To appear before a federal court, an attorney requires specific admission to that court's bar.

A fundamental tenet of counsel's duty in some common law countries (but not, surprisingly, in the United States) is the so-called 'cab-rank rule' under which 'no counsel is entitled to refuse to act in a sphere in which he or she practises, and on being tendered a proper fee, for any person however unpopular or offensive he or his opinions may be'. Like a taxi driver who is generally obliged to accept any passenger, a barrister is bound to accept any brief unless there are circumstances to justify a refusal, such as that the area of law lies outside of his expertise or experience, or where his professional commitments prevent him from devoting sufficient time to the case.

In the absence of such a rule, advocates would be reluctant to appear on behalf of abhorrent, immoral, or malevolent clients charged, for example, with heinous crimes such as child molestation. Nevertheless, in practice it is not difficult for a barrister to find a reason why the brief should not be accepted. Apart from the case involving an area of law beyond his or her capability, the human element is always present: time is more easily found for a lucrative brief than one which concerns an intractable or hopeless case. But it represents a sound statement of professional duty, emphasizing the role of lawyer as 'hired gun' who acts fearlessly for any client regardless of the merits of their case.

A striking feature of the training of common lawyers has been the role of some form of apprenticeship (see later in the chapter). Indeed, it was only towards the end of the 19th century that English universities taught any law at all. And large-scale university legal education in the United States, Canada, Australia, and New Zealand had to await the 20th century, though some universities had established law schools earlier (notably Harvard in 1817).

Civil lawyers

Lawyers in the civil law world differ fundamentally from their common law colleagues. Indeed, the very concept of a legal profession in the major civil law jurisdictions of Europe, Latin America, Japan, and Scandinavia is problematic. In the words of a leading authority on the subject, 'The common law folk concept of "lawyer" has no counterpart in European languages.' Civil law jurisdictions recognize two categories of legal professionals: the jurist and the private practitioner. The former comprises law graduates, while the latter, unlike the position in common law countries, does not represent the nucleus of the legal profession. Instead, 'other subsets of law graduates take precedence—historically, numerically, and ideologically. These include the magistracy (judges and prosecutors)...civil servants, law professors, and lawyers employed in commerce and industry.'

Students in civil law countries typically decide on their future after graduation. And, as mobility within the profession is limited, in many jurisdictions this choice is likely to be conclusive. They may choose to pursue the career of a judge, a public prosecutor, a government lawyer, an advocate, or notary. *Private* practice is therefore generally divided between advocates and notaries. The former has direct contact with clients and represents them in court. After graduating from law school, advocates normally serve an apprenticeship with experienced lawyers for a number of years, and then tend to practise as sole practitioners or in small firms.

To become a notary usually requires passing a state examination. Notaries draft legal documents such as wills and contracts, authenticate such documents in legal proceedings, and maintain records on, or provide copies of, authenticated documents. Government lawyers serve either as public prosecutors or as lawyers for government agencies. The public prosecutor performs a twin function. In criminal cases, he or she prepares the government's case; while in certain civil cases they represent the public interest.

In most civil law jurisdictions, the state plays a considerably more important role in the training, entry, and employment of lawyers than is the case in the common law world. Unlike the traditional position in common law countries where lawyers qualify by serving an apprenticeship, the state controls the number of jurists it will employ, and the universities mediate entry into private practice.

There are important differences between the two systems in respect of the organization of legal education. Broadly speaking, in most common law jurisdictions (with the conspicuous exception of England and Hong Kong), law is a postgraduate degree or, as in Australia, New Zealand, and Canada, it may be combined with an undergraduate degree in another discipline. In the civil law world, on the other hand, law is an undergraduate course. While the common law curriculum is strongly influenced by the legal profession, the state in civil law jurisdictions exercises a dominant function in this respect. The legal profession in most common law countries administers entry examinations, whereas, given the role of universities as gatekeepers in civil law countries, further examinations are generally redundant, and a law degree suffices.

The function of gatekeeping in common law countries tends to be discharged by apprenticeship with a private practitioner. So, for example, aspiring barristers must pass the bar examinations. In order to practise at the bar, they are required to serve two six-month pupillages in chambers, attending conferences with solicitors conducted by their 'pupil master' (a more senior barrister), and sitting in court, assisting in preparing cases, drafting opinions, and so on. Pupillage is usually unpaid, although they are now increasingly funded so as to guarantee the pupil's earnings up to a fixed level. During the second six months of pupillage, the barrister may engage in limited practice and be instructed in his or her own right. With the exception of barristers, lawyers in private practice operate as members of a firm whose size may vary from a single lawyer to mega-firms of hundreds of lawyers.

Regulation of the profession

Bar associations, bar councils, and law societies are among the numerous organizations that supervise the admission, licensing, education, and regulation of common lawyers. The civil law prefers the term 'advocates' (which more accurately describes their principal function, and their counterpart organizations are dubbed chambers, orders, faculties, or colleges of advocates). Although their designations differ, they generally share a concern to limit the number of lawyers in practice, and defend their monopoly.

In certain jurisdictions (particularly small ones like Belgium and New Zealand), lawyers are admitted and regulated at the national level. Federal states (such as the United States, Canada, Australia, and Germany) inevitably exercise provincial or state regulation. Italian lawyers are admitted at the regional level.

While regulation in some countries is undertaken by the judiciary and, under its aegis, an independent legal profession, lawyers in other jurisdictions, especially in the civil law world, are subject to government control in the shape of the ministry of justice.

Legal aid

The right of access to justice rings hollow without the provision of free legal advice and assistance to the poor, especially in criminal cases. Many societies therefore grant legal aid to persons incapable of paying for a lawyer. Even in respect of civil litigation, however, elementary norms of fairness would be undermined where an impecunious defendant is sued by an affluent plaintiff or the state. Any semblance of equality before the law is thereby shattered. The cost involved (to both the state and the individual seeking legal aid) generally results in preference being given to assisting those charged with criminal offences, though some jurisdictions do supply free legal aid in civil cases. Certain systems of legal aid provide lawyers who are employed exclusively to act for eligible, impoverished clients. Others appoint private practitioners to represent such individuals.

The United States Supreme Court in the landmark case of *Gideon v Wainwright* in 1963 unanimously ruled that states are constitutionally obliged to provide counsel in criminal cases to represent defendants who are unable to afford them. These so-called 'public defenders' may be appointed by the court to assist and represent indigent individuals, but their efficacy is often compromised by their youth, inexperience, and excessive workload.

Unrepresented defendants in criminal trials are at a considerable disadvantage. Without legal aid, the poor are denied their right to equality before the law and to a fair trial. As the Supreme Court declared in *Gideon*:

> [R]eason and reflection require us to recognize that in our adversary system of criminal justice, any person haled into court, who is too poor to hire a lawyer, cannot be assured a fair trial unless counsel is provided for him. This seems to us to be an obvious truth...This noble ideal cannot be realized if the poor man charged with crime has to face his accusers without a lawyer to assist him.

Sadly, this 'noble ideal' remains in many countries just that.

Chapter 6
The future of the law

Law, like war, seems to be an inescapable fact of the human condition. But what is its future? The law is, of course, in a constant state of flux. This is nicely expressed by the illustrious American Supreme Court Justice Benjamin Cardozo:

> Existing rules and principles can give us our present location, our bearings, our latitude and longitude. The inn that shelters us for the night is not the journey's end. The law, like the traveller, must be ready for the morrow. It must have a principle of growth.

In our rapidly changing world, growth and adaptation are more pressing than ever if the law is to respond adequately to the novel challenges—and threats—that it faces. The character of law has unquestionably undergone profound transformations in the last fifty years, yet its future is uncertain. Some argue that the law is in its death throes, while others advance a different prognosis that discerns numerous signs of law's enduring strength. Which is it? Curiously, there is some truth in both standpoints.

Those who suggest that law is moribund point to signs of the infirmity of many advanced legal systems. Symptoms of this demise include the privatization of law: the settlement of cases out of court, plea-bargaining, ADR, the spectacular rise of regulatory agencies with wide discretionary powers, and the decline of the rule of law in several countries.

On the other hand, the resilience of law is evident in the extension of the law's tentacles into the private domain in pursuit of efficiency, social justice, and other political goals; the globalization of law and its internationalization through the United Nations, regional organizations, and the European Union; and the massive impact of technology on the law.

This concluding chapter attempts to uncover some of the major shifts in contemporary society and the formidable challenges they pose to the law.

Law and change

Various attempts have been made to chart the course of legal development. Legal historians have sought to identify the central features in the evolution of law, and, hence, to place different societies along this continuum. In the late 19th century, the eminent scholar Sir Henry Maine famously contended that law and society had previously progressed 'from status to contract'. In other words, in the ancient world individuals were closely bound by status to traditional groups, whereas in modern societies individuals are regarded as autonomous beings—they are free to enter into contracts and form associations with whomever they choose.

But this transition may have reversed. In many instances freedom of contract is more apparent than real. For example, what choice does the consumer have when faced with a standard-form contract (or contract of adhesion) for telecommunications, electricity, or other utilities? And where is the employee who, when offered a job and presented with a standard-form contract by his multinational employee, would attempt to renegotiate the terms? It is true that many advanced legal systems seek to improve the bargaining position of the individual through various forms of consumer protection legislation. Yet when a lightweight steps into the ring with a heavyweight, the outcome is rarely in doubt. Has 'status' returned in the form of 'consumer' or 'employee'?

The ideas of the German social theorist, Max Weber, have exerted a powerful influence on thinking about law and its development. He advanced a 'typology' of law based on the different categories of legal thought. At its heart is the idea of 'rationality'. He distinguishes between 'formal' systems and 'substantive' systems. The core of this division is the extent to which a system is 'internally self-sufficient', i.e. the rules and procedures required for decision making are available within the system. Second, he separates 'rational' from 'irrational' systems. 'Rationality' refers to the manner in which legal rules and procedures are applied. The highest stage of rationality is reached when all legal propositions constitute a logically clear, internally consistent system of rules under which every conceivable fact or situation is included.

Weber gives as an example of a formally legal irrational system the phenomenon of trial by ordeal where guilt is determined by an appeal to some supernatural force. An illustration of substantive legal irrationality is where a judge decides a case on the basis of his personal opinion without any reference to rules. A decision of a judge is substantively rational, according to Weber, when he refers not to rules but moral principles or concepts of justice. Finally, where a judge defers to a body of doctrine consisting of legal rules and principles, the system constitutes one of formal logical legal rationality. It is towards this ideal type that Weber's theory of legal evolution progresses.

In many societies, however, Weber's model of a rational, comprehensive, and coherent legal system is undermined by the rapid rise in administrative control. Contemporary societies manifest an enormous expansion in the jurisdiction of administrative agencies. These bodies, normally creatures of statute, are vested with extensive discretionary powers. In some cases, their decisions are explicitly exempted from judicial oversight.

In several European countries, for example, the privatization of formerly nationalized industries (such as utilities and telecommunications) has spawned a host of regulatory agencies with powers to investigate, create rules, and impose penalties. The ordinary courts may be marginalized, and hence the role of law itself becomes distorted. This development poses a threat to the authority and openness of the court system described in Chapter 4. Moreover, the enlargement of discretionary powers undermines the rule of law's insistence on the observance of clear rules that specify individual rights and duties.

Disappearing law?

Among the more radical theories of legal development is the Marxist idea that law is doomed to disappear completely. This prediction is grounded in the idea of historicism: social evolution is explained as a movement driven by inexorable historical forces. Marx and Engels propounded the theory of 'dialectical materialism', which explains the unfolding of history as the development of a thesis, its opposite (or antithesis), and, out of the ensuing conflict, its resolution in a synthesis.

Marx argued that each period of economic development has a corresponding class system. During the period of hand-mill production, for instance, the feudal system of classes existed. When steam-mill production developed, capitalism replaced feudalism. Classes are determined by the means of production, and therefore an individual's class is dependent on his relation to the means of production. Marx's 'historical materialism' is based on the fact that the means of production are materially determined; it is dialectical, in part, because he sees an inevitable conflict between those two hostile classes. A revolution would eventually occur because the bourgeois mode of production based on individual ownership and unplanned competition, stands in opposition to the increasingly non-individualistic, social character of labour production in the factory.

The proletariat would, he predicted, seize the means of production and establish a 'dictatorship of the proletariat' which would, in time, be replaced by a classless, communist society in which law would eventually 'wither away'. Since the law is a vehicle of class oppression, it is superfluous in a classless society. This is the essence of the argument first implied by Marx in his early writings and restated by Lenin. In its more sophisticated version the thesis claims that, following the proletarian revolution, the bourgeois state would be swept aside and replaced by the dictatorship of the proletariat. Society, after reactionary resistance has been defeated, would have no further need for law or state: they would vanish.

But this cheerful prognosis is based on a rather crude equation of law with the coercive suppression of the proletariat. It disregards the fact not only that a considerable body of law serves other functions, but that even, or especially, a communist society requires laws to plan and regulate the economy. To claim that these measures are not 'law' is to invite disbelief.

Whatever theory is adopted to explain the manner and form of legal change, it is impossible to deny that the future of law is beset with a host of thorny challenges. Where might the greatest difficulties lie?

Internal challenges

In addition to the problem of bureaucratic regulation and the often unbridled discretion it generates (discussed earlier), there are a number of intractable questions that need to be confronted by legal systems. Some of these were touched on in Chapters 2 and 3. Among the most conspicuous is the increasing threat of terrorism by extremist groups in several countries. It requires little perception to realize that many legal systems are faced with a variety of problems that test the values that lie at their heart. How can a free society reconcile a commitment to liberty with the necessity to confront threats to undermine that very foundation? Absolute security is clearly unattainable, but even moderate protection against terror comes at a price. No airline passenger can be unaware of the cost in respect of the delays and inconvenience that today's security checks inevitably entail.

Nevertheless, although terrorism and crime in general can never be entirely prevented, modern technology does offer extraordinarily successful tools to deter and apprehend offenders. At the most commonplace level, closed-circuit television (CCTV) cameras can monitor unlawful activities, such recordings supplying prosecutors with powerful evidence in court against the videoed villain. To what extent should the law tolerate this kind of surveillance?

Surely, most delinquents would be thwarted were a CCTV camera to record his (or, less likely, her) every move? Law-abiding citizens must feel safer in the knowledge that this surveillance is taking place. Indeed, opinion polls confirm their wide support. Who but the robber, abductor, or bomber has anything to fear from the monitoring of his or her activities in public places? Advances in technology render the tracking of an individual's financial transactions and email communications simple. The introduction of 'smart' ID cards, the use of biometrics, and electronic road pricing are now routine. Only the malevolent could legitimately object to these effective methods of crime control. Would that this comforting view were true.

We cannot afford to pussyfoot with terrorists, but how far should we be willing to trade our freedom for security? In the immediate aftermath of the events of 11 September 2001, politicians, especially in the United States, have understandably sought to enhance the powers of the state to detain suspects for interrogation, intercept communications, and monitor the activities of those who might be engaged in terrorism.

The recent revelations by former US government contractor and whistle-blower, Edward Snowden, exposed the considerable extent of the surveillance conducted by the US National Security Agency (NSA). They included disclosures of spying by both the US and Britain on foreign leaders, and the storage by the NSA of domestic communications containing foreign intelligence information; the suggestion of a crime; threats of serious harm to life or property; or any other evidence that could advance its electronic surveillance—including encrypted communications. Moreover, it emerged that, since December 2012, the NSA has had the capacity to collect a trillion metadata records. Other leaks suggested that the US had spied on the European Union (EU) offices in New York, Washington, DC, and Brussels, as well as the embassies of France, Greece, India, Italy, Japan, Mexico, South Korea, and Turkey.

Evidence also appeared to show the existence of an NSA project to collect information from the fibre optic cables that carry most Internet and phone traffic. And it discloses the existence of a programme comprising a network of 500 servers scattered across the world that collect almost all online activities conducted by a user, storing the information in databases searchable by name, email, IP address, region, and language. It also divulged that the private sector, including several telecom companies, provide the British security agency, GCHQ, with unrestricted access to their fibre optic cable networks, carrying a vast quantity of Internet and telephone traffic.

In addition, according to the leaks, the NSA has cracked the encryption methods widely used by millions of individuals and organizations to protect their email, e-commerce, and financial transactions. It is also alleged that the NSA employs its colossal databases to store metadata, such as email correspondence, online searches, and the browsing history of millions of Internet users for up to a year, regardless of whether they are targets of the agency.

The threat of terrorism cannot be taken lightly, but unless individual privacy is to be wholly extinguished, the effective oversight of security services is crucial. In March 2014, President Obama announced that the NSA's bulk collection of Americans' telephone records would be terminated. In June 2015 the powers of the NSA to collect telephone data were curbed.

The law faces formidable difficulties in this respect. Draconian powers are probably unavoidable during times of war: arbitrary powers of arrest and detention, imprisonment without trial, secret trials, and the like. How long can a free society tolerate these infringements of liberty? What lasting damage may be inflicted on the rule of law and individual rights? Can the law continue to protect citizens or will citizens need protection *from* the law? Are the courts able to act as a bulwark against these attacks on freedom?

In Chapter 3, the question of the use of torture was discussed. Can it be justified in order to prevent acts of terror? Methods used by the CIA, we saw, were described in a recent contentious senate report as brutal and ineffective, and a blemish on American values. Several reports of the torture of detainees at the US Guantanamo Bay camp have emerged over the years. The treatment of these individuals (most of whom were captured in Afghanistan) has been strongly condemned as inhumane, in breach of international law, and a denial of the detainees' legal rights including *habeas corpus* and access to legal counsel.

There can be little doubt that the law will be placed under growing pressure as it strives to reconcile freedom with the perils of terrorism and extremism that threaten to destroy the values cherished by democratic legal systems (see Box 14).

Box 14 Terrorism and freedom

We need not sacrifice our constitutional freedoms to win the Wars on Terror. Indeed...twenty-first century terrorism poses a danger to those freedoms. Claims that the U.S. Constitution doesn't apply abroad, or that habeas corpus is a quaint irrelevance, or that persons can be held incommunicado indefinitely, are ones with which I have little sympathy. But neither do I believe that there is a God-given right to not be burdened with carrying an identity card, or to not disclose to the government information we have gladly given to private corporations or that they have collected with our consent.

Philip Bobbitt, *Terror and Consent*

A less egregious engine of change is the internationalization or globalization of law. The world has witnessed an escalation in the influence and importance of international (the United Nations) or regional organizations (such as the EU). These sources of law diminish the authority of domestic law and legal institutions. Nor has the law been spared the McDonald's effect of powerful multinational corporations influencing the character of banking, investments, consumer markets, and so on. All have a direct impact on the law.

It is hard to think of a single facet of law that is untouched by globalization (or what is called the internationalization of law). From the development of transnational commerce, markets, and banking to the growing number of problems faced by international law, including, for instance, climate change, international human rights violations, terrorism, and piracy.

Most legal systems face unresolved dilemmas in several of the disciplines discussed in Chapter 2, where I touched upon some of these problems. They are both substantive and procedural, and include several quandaries concerning, to mention only one of countless possible examples, the criminal justice system. What is the future of the criminal trial in the face of complex commercial offences, often involving sophisticated know-how? Is the jury trial appropriate in these circumstances, or at all? Is the civil law inquisitorial system preferable to the common law adversarial approach?

Corruption is a scourge that legal systems need to address. In several jurisdictions, access to the law is patchy. The poor are not always provided with adequate access to the courts and other institutions of dispute resolution. Many legal systems wrestle with the difficult question of compensation for personal injuries, and the effect of insurance on the award of damages. The Internet and other technological developments generate a multiplicity of legal challenges. Some are considered in what follows.

The limits of law

While the law on its own can never transform, or indeed conserve, the social order and its values, it has the capacity to influence and shape attitudes. Efforts to achieve social justice through law have not been an unqualified success. Statutes outlawing racial discrimination, for example, represent only a modest advance in the cause of equality. While little can be accomplished *without* legal intervention, the limits of law need to be acknowledged. There is a growing tendency to legalize moral and social problems, and even to assume that the values underpinning democratic Western legal systems, and their institutions, can be fruitfully exported or transplanted to less developed countries. This may be a utopian vision. Equally sanguine may be the suggestion that economic development necessarily presages respect for human rights, as is frequently contended in the case of China.

Modern governments espouse highly ambitious legislative programmes that frequently verge upon social engineering. To what extent can legislation genuinely improve society, and combat discrimination and injustice? Or are courts more appropriate vehicles for social change? Where, as in the United States, a vigorous Supreme Court has the clout to declare laws unconstitutional, the legislature has no choice but to fall in line, as it did following the seminal case of *Brown v Board of Education of Topeka* in 1954. A unanimous court declared the establishment of separate public schools for black and white students 'inherently unequal'. This landmark decision opened the doors (literally) to integration and the birth of the civil rights movement. Though discrimination will always exist, few would deny that the court's historic decision changed the law—and society—for the better.

Without effective enforcement, laws cannot fulfil their noble aspirations. Legislation prohibiting animal cruelty is a case in point (see Figure 11). Vivisection, battery farming, animal transport, the fur trade, hunting, trapping, circuses, some zoos, and rodeos are merely some of the practices, apart from the direct intentional infliction of pain on an animal, that cause misery and suffering to millions of creatures around the world every day.

11. **Protest against animal cruelty.**

Anti-cruelty statutes have been enacted in many jurisdictions, yet in the absence of rigorous enforcement these laws constitute mostly empty promises. And enforcement is a major hurdle: detection is largely dependent on inspectors who lack the power of arrest, prosecutors who rarely regard animal cruelty cases as a high priority, and judges who seldom impose adequate punishment, not that the statutory penalty is itself sufficiently stringent (see Boxes 15 and 16).

In an increasingly anxious world, there is an understandable tendency to look to the law to resolve the manifold threats to our future. In recent years, the dangers of pollution, depletion of the ozone layer, global warming, and other threats to the survival of many species of animal, marine, bird, and plant life have assumed greater importance and urgency. A growing number of nations have introduced legislation to attempt to limit or control the destruction of the planet. The law, however, often proves to be a rather blunt instrument. For example, in the case of the criminal liability of a company for pollution, a conviction depends on proof that those who control the company had the requisite knowledge or intention. This is notoriously difficult to prove. And even where these acts are strict liability offences, the fines imposed by courts have a limited deterrent effect. It may be that the numerous international treaties, conventions, and declarations on almost every aspect of environmental protection are likely to be more effective, though, as with the law the predictable stumbling block is effective implementation.

Box 15 Da Vinci's code

The time will come when people such as I will look upon the murder of (other) animals as they now look upon the murder of human beings.

Leonardo da Vinci

Box 16 The law and animal suffering

The day may come, when the rest of the animal creation may acquire those rights which never could have been withholden from them but by the hand of tyranny. The French have already discovered that the blackness of skin is no reason why a human being should be abandoned without redress to the caprice of a tormentor. It may come one day to be recognized, that the number of legs, the villosity of the skin, or the termination of the os sacrum, are reasons equally insufficient for abandoning a sensitive being to the same fate. What else is it that should trace the insuperable line? Is it the faculty of reason, or perhaps, the faculty for discourse? . . . [T]he question is not, Can they reason? nor, Can they talk? but, Can they suffer? Why should the law refuse its protection to any sensitive being? . . . The time will come when humanity will extend its mantle over everything which breathes . . .

Jeremy Bentham, *Introduction to the Principles of Morals and Legislation*

Law and injustice

The law may, of course, be the source of injustice. As mentioned in Chapter 3, apartheid was a creature of the law. And the same can be said of the atrocities of the Third Reich. And sometimes courts are guilty of injustice. The infamous Dreyfus affair in France is a striking example of the conviction and punishment of an innocent person as a result of a combination of incompetence and anti-Semitism. Though Dreyfus was eventually exonerated, the case demonstrates how even judges may be susceptible to bigotry and prejudice.

The American Supreme Court has not been immune from unjust decisions. In one of its most notorious cases it decided against

Dred Scott, a slave who in 1847 applied to a court to obtain his freedom. The judges ruled that no person of African origin could ever become a citizen of the United States, and Scott therefore had no right to bring his case. It also held that the government lacked the power to prohibit slavery.

No less dishonourable was the court's judgment in *Plessy v Ferguson* in 1896 which upheld the constitutionality of racial segregation in public facilities under the 'separate but equal' doctrine. It took more than half a century for the court to overrule this decision in their celebrated *Brown* decision mentioned earlier.

In 1991 in Los Angeles the case of Rodney King sparked riots after the acquittal of police officers who had struck him up to fifty-six times with metal batons, kicked him, and shot him with a Taser stun gun. A number of bystanders witnessed the beating, one of whom videotaped the incident. King suffered a fractured skull and nerve damage to his face. Though some of the officers were subsequently convicted by a federal court on charges of violating King's constitutional rights, and imprisoned, none of the prosecutions specifically alleged racial motivation. The police shooting of black suspects and the failure to prosecute the alleged offenders remains a highly volatile issue in the United States.

We should not be surprised that miscarriages of justice occur. Courts are not infallible, and there is always the possibility of errors, oversights, and contaminated or false evidence that can lead to the conviction of an innocent defendant. One of the strongest arguments against capital punishment is founded on this terrible prospect.

Technological challenges

There is nothing new about the law's struggle to keep abreast with technology. Yet the last twenty years have witnessed an unprecedented transformation of the contest. Digital disquiet casily spawns alarm and anxiety. Information technology, to select only one obvious instance, poses enormous challenges to the law. Attempts legally to control the Internet, its operation, or content, have been notoriously unsuccessful. Indeed, its very anarchy and resistance to regulation is, in the minds of many, its strength and attraction. But is cyberspace beyond regulation? Professor Lawrence Lessig has cogently argued that it is indeed susceptible to control, not necessarily by law, but through its essential make-up, its 'code': software and hardware that constitute cyberspace. That code, he suggests, can either produce a place where freedom prevails or one of oppressive control.

In fact, commercial considerations increasingly render cyberspace decidedly amenable to regulation; it has become a place in which conduct is more strongly controlled than in real space. In the end, Lessig maintains, it is a matter for us to determine; the choice is one of architecture: what sort of code should govern cyberspace, and who will control it? And in this respect, the central legal issue is code. We need to choose the values and principles which should animate that code.

Information is no longer merely power. It is big business. In recent years, the fastest growing component of international trade is the service sector. It accounts for more than one-third of world trade—and continues to expand. It is common to identify, as a central feature of modern industrialized societies, their dependence on the storage of information. The use of computers facilitates, of course, considerably greater efficiency and velocity in the collection, storage, retrieval, and transfer of information. The everyday functions of the state as well as private bodies require a continual supply of data about individuals in order to administer effectively the numerous services that are integral to contemporary life and the expectations of citizens. Thus, to mention only the most conspicuous examples, the provision of health care, social security, and the prevention and detection of crime by law enforcement authorities assume the accessibility of a vast quantity of such data, and, hence, a willingness of the public to furnish them. Equally in the private sector, the provision of credit, insurance, and employment generate an almost insatiable hunger for information.

Big brother?

Can the law control the seemingly relentless slide towards an Orwellian nightmare? 'Low-tech' collection of transactional data in both the public and private sector has become commonplace. In addition to the routine surveillance by CCTV in public places, the monitoring of mobile telephones, the workplace, vehicles, electronic communications, and online activity are increasingly taken for granted in most advanced societies. The privacy prognosis is not encouraging; the future promises more sophisticated and alarming intrusions into our private lives, including the greater use of biometrics, and sense-enhanced searches such as satellite monitoring, and penetrating walls and clothing.

As cyberspace becomes an increasingly perilous domain, we learn daily of new, alarming assaults on its citizens. This slide towards pervasive surveillance coincides with the mounting fears, expressed well before 9/11, about the disturbing capacity of the new technology to undermine our liberty. Reports of the fragility of privacy have, of course, been sounded for at least a century. But in the last decade they have assumed a more urgent form.

And here lies a paradox. On the one hand, recent advances in the power of computers have been decried as the nemesis of whatever vestiges of our privacy still survive. On the other, the Internet is acclaimed as a utopia. When clichés contend, it is imprudent to expect sensible resolutions of the problems they embody, but between these two exaggerated claims, something resembling the truth probably resides. In respect of the future of privacy, at least, there can be little doubt that the legal questions are changing before our eyes. And if, in the flat-footed domain of atoms, we have achieved only limited success in protecting individuals against the depredations of surveillance, how much better the prospects in our brave new binary world?

In 2010 the now famous (or infamous) international, online, journalistic NGO (non-governmental organization), WikiLeaks, led by Julian Assange, began releasing a huge number of documents relating mainly to the wars in Afghanistan and Iraq. Towards the end of that year it released almost 400,000 secret United States military logs detailing its operations in Iraq, and it collaborated with several media organizations to disclose US State Department diplomatic cables. In 2013, Bradley (now Chelsea) Manning, a twenty-five-year-old soldier, was convicted of twenty charges in connection with the leaks, including espionage, and sentenced to thirty-five years' imprisonment.

But the activities of WikiLeaks, though continuing, were eclipsed by the massive revelations in June 2013 by a former US government contractor, Edward Snowden. In a dramatic sequence of whistle-blowing, he revealed the enormous extent of the surveillance conducted by the NSA. It disclosed that the NSA was collecting the telephone records of tens of millions of Americans. This was soon followed by evidence that the NSA had direct access—via the PRISM programme—to the servers of several major tech companies, including Apple, Google, and Microsoft.

The constitutionality of the NSA's mass collection of telephone phone records recently restricted by a change in the law, as already mentioned, has now been challenged by the American Civil Liberties Union (ACLU). The complaint contends that the dragnet under the Patriot Act infringes the right of privacy protected by the Fourth Amendment, as well as the First Amendment rights of free speech and association. The lawsuit seeks to terminate the

NSA's mass domestic surveillance, and to require the deletion of all data collected. A federal judge denied the ACLU's motion for a preliminary injunction, and granted the government's motion to dismiss. The ACLU appealed this decision before the US Court of Appeals for the Second Circuit in New York.

When our security is under siege, so—inevitably—is our liberty. A world in which our every movement is observed erodes the very freedom this snooping is often calculated to protect. Naturally, we need to ensure that the social costs of the means employed to enhance security do not outweigh the benefits. Thus, one unsurprising consequence of the installation of CCTV in car parks, shopping malls, airports, and other public places is the displacement of crime; offenders simply go somewhere else. And, apart from the doors this intrusion opens to totalitarianism, a surveillance society can easily generate a climate of mistrust and suspicion, a reduction in the respect for law and those who enforce it, and an intensification of prosecution of offences that are susceptible to easy detection and proof.

European data protection legislation attempts to regulate the collection and use of personal information. But the law is locked in an unceasing struggle to stay ahead of advancing technology. At the heart of the law is the modest proposition that data relating to an identifiable individual should not be collected in the absence of a genuine purpose and the consent of the individual concerned. The new information technology disintegrates national borders; international traffic in personal data is a routine feature of commercial life. The protection afforded to personal data in Country A is, in a digital world, rendered nugatory when it is retrieved on a computer in Country B in which there are no controls over its use. Hence, states with data protection laws frequently proscribe the transfer of data to countries that lack them. Indeed, the EU has in one of its several directives explicitly sought to annihilate these 'data havens'. Without data protection legislation, countries risk being shut out of the rapidly expanding information business.

At the core of these laws are two central canons of fair information practice that speak for themselves: the 'use limitation' and 'purpose specification' principles. They require rejuvenation where they already exist, and urgent adoption where they do not (most conspicuously, and indefensibly, in the United States). They may, moreover, be able to provide complementary safeguards for individual privacy in cyberspace.

Developments in biotechnology such as human cloning, embryo stem cell research, genetic engineering, GM crops, and nanotechnology provoke thorny ethical questions and confront traditional legal concepts. Proposals to introduce identity cards and biometrics have attracted strong objections in several jurisdictions. The nature of criminal trials has been transformed by the use of both DNA and CCTV evidence.

Orwellian supervision already appears to be alive and well in several countries. Britain, for example, boasts more than four million CCTV cameras in public places: roughly one for every fourteen inhabitants. It also possesses the world's largest DNA database, comprising some 5.3 million DNA samples. The temptation to install CCTV cameras by both the public and private sector is not easy to resist. The boundary between the state and business is disintegrating. Information is routinely shared between the two. For example, Google may provide user data when subject to a court order. Or even without it. It is claimed that in the US lucrative provisions exist by which the state outsources data gathering to ten major telecommunications companies, including AT&T, Verizon, and T-Mobile who reaped considerable sums of money supplying law enforcement authorities with personal telecom information.

More disturbing, however, is the scale of the systematic collection of personal data by major websites such as Google, Facebook, and Amazon. And they frequently comply with government requests for consumers' personal information. In fact, the capture of such data is fundamental to the business models of the most successful technology firms, and they are increasingly permeating traditional activities such as retail business, health care, finance, entertainment and the media, and insurance. Companies such as PayPal and Visa track online transactions. Google and other agencies obtain private information by cookies and 'click-throughs'. And so-called private data aggregators collect personal data which they then sell.

These are merely random examples of what has been described as an arms race between privacy-enhancing technology (PETS) and privacy-invading technology (PITS). It is too early to predict which side will triumph.

The future of the right to privacy depends in large part on the ability of the law to formulate an adequately clear definition of the concept itself. This is not only a consequence of the inherent vagueness of the notion of privacy, but also because the 'right of privacy' has conspicuously failed to provide adequate support to the private realm when it is intruded upon by competing rights and interests, especially freedom of expression. In our burgeoning information age, the vulnerability of privacy is likely to intensify unless this central democratic value is translated into simple language that is capable of effective regulation.

Other developments have comprehensively altered fundamental features of the legal landscape. The law has been profoundly affected and challenged by numerous other advances in technology. Computer fraud, identity theft, and other cybercrimes, and the pirating of digital music, are examples.

A recent development in the field of data collection and storage is the advent of so-called 'big data', used to describe the exponential increase and availability of data. It is characterized by what has been called the 'three Vs': volume, velocity, and variety. In respect of the first, the volume is a consequence of the ease of storage of transaction-based data, unstructured data streaming in from social media, and the accumulation of sensor and machine-to-machine data. Second, data are streamed at high velocity from radio frequency identification (RFID) tags, sensors, and smart metering. And third, data assume a multiplicity of forms including structured, numeric data in traditional databases, from line-of-business applications, unstructured text documents, video, audio, email, and financial transactions.

Its advocates claim that it affords opportunities to correlate data in order to combat crime, prevent disease, forecast weather patterns, identify business trends, and so on. Its detractors question the reliability of its correlations, and the interpretation of the results.

New wrongs and rights

Advances in technology are predictably accompanied by new forms of mischief. The law is not always the most effective or appropriate instrument to deploy against these novel depredations. Technology itself frequently offers superior solutions. In the case of the Internet, for example, a variety of measures exist to protect personal data online. These include the encryption, economization, and erasure of personal data.

While new-fangled wrongs will continue to emerge, some transgressions are simply digital versions of old ones. Among the more obvious novel threats, there are a number which tease the law's capacity to respond to new offences. These include complex problems arising largely from the ease with which data, software, or music may be copied. The pillars upon which intellectual property law was constructed have been shaken. This incorporates the law of patents and trademarks, especially in respect of domain names. Defective software gives rise to potential contractual and tortious claims for compensation. The storage of data on mobile telephones and other devices persistently tests the law's ability to protect the innocent against the 'theft' of information. New threats emerge almost daily.

Criminals have not been slow to exploit the law's frailties. Cybercrime poses new challenges for criminal justice, criminal law, and law enforcement both nationally and internationally. Innovative online criminals generate major headaches for police, prosecutors, and courts. This new terrain incorporates cybercrimes against the person (such as cyberstalking and cyberpornography), and cybercrimes against property (such as hacking, viruses, causing damage to data), cyberfraud, identity theft, and cyberterrorism. Cyberspace provides organized crime with more sophisticated and potentially more secure methods for supporting and developing networks for a range of criminal activities, including drug and arms trafficking, money laundering, and smuggling.

Some wrongs have simply undergone a digital rebirth. For example, the tort of defamation has found a congenial new habitat in cyberspace. The law in most jurisdictions protects the reputation of persons through the tort of defamation or its equivalent. It will be recalled that while there are variations within common law jurisdictions, the law generally imposes liability where the defendant intentionally or negligently publishes a false, unprivileged statement of fact that harms the plaintiff's reputation. Civil law systems, instead of recognizing a separate head tort of defamation, protect reputation under the wing of rights of the personality. In cyberspace, however, national borders tend to disintegrate, and such distinctions lose much of their importance.

The advent of email, Facebook, Twitter, bulletin boards, newsgroups, and blogs provide fertile ground for defamatory statements online. Since the law normally requires publication to only one person other than the victim, an email message or posting on a newsgroup will suffice to found liability. But it is not merely the author of the libel who may be liable.

Law in a precarious world

As it unfolds, the 21st century yields few reasons to be cheerful. Our world continues to be blighted by war, genocide, poverty, disease, corruption, bigotry, and greed. More than one-sixth of its inhabitants—over a billion people—live on less than $1 a day. Over 800 million go to bed hungry every night, representing 14 per cent of the world's population. The United Nations estimates that hunger claims the lives of about 25,000 people every day. The relationship between poverty and disease is unambiguous. In respect of HIV/AIDS, for example, 95 per cent of cases occur in developing countries. Two-thirds of the forty million people infected with HIV live in sub-Saharan Africa.

Amid these gloomy statistics, occasional shafts of light appear to justify optimism. There has been some progress in diminishing at least some of the inequality and injustice that afflict individuals and groups in many parts of the world. And this has been, in no small measure, an important achievement of the law. It is easy, and always fashionable, to disparage the law, and especially lawyers, for neglecting—or even aggravating—the world's misery. Yet such cynicism is increasingly unfounded in the light of the progress, albeit lumbering, in the legal recognition and protection of human rights.

The adoption by the United Nations, in the grim shadow of the Holocaust, of the Universal Declaration of Human Rights in 1948, and the International Covenants on Civil and Political Rights, and Economic, Social and Cultural Rights in 1976, demonstrates, even to the most sceptical observer, a commitment by the international community to the universal conception and protection of human rights. As mentioned earlier, this so-called International Bill of Rights, with its inevitably protean and slightly kaleidoscopic ideological character, reflects an extraordinary measure of cross-cultural consensus among nations.

The idea of human rights has passed through three generations. The first generation consisted of mostly 'negative' civil and political rights. A right is negative in the sense that it entails a right not to be interfered with in certain prohibited ways, for example my right to speak freely. A right is positive, on the other hand, when it expresses a claim to something such as education or health or legal representation. These second-generation rights crowd under the umbrella of economic, social, and cultural rights.

The third generation of rights comprises primarily collective rights which are foreshadowed in Article 28 of the Universal Declaration, which declares that 'everyone is entitled to a social and international order in which the rights set forth in this Declaration can be fully realized'. These 'solidarity' rights include the right to social and economic development and to participate in and benefit from the resources of the earth and space, the right to scientific and technical information (which are especially important to the Third World), and the right to a healthy environment, peace, and humanitarian disaster relief (see Figure 12).

It is sometimes contended that unwarranted primacy is given to positive rights at the expense of negative rights. The latter, it is argued, are the 'genuine' human rights, since without food, water, and shelter, the former are a luxury. The reality, however, is that both sets of rights are equally important. Democratic governments that respect free speech are more likely to address the needs of the poor. On the other hand, in societies where economic and social rights are protected, democracy has an enhanced prospect of success since people are not preoccupied with concerns about their next meal.

Misgivings surrounding the concept of human rights are not new. Qualms are expressed by those who perceive the expanding recognition of human rights as undermining the 'war on terror'. Still others find many of the rights expressed in declarations to be

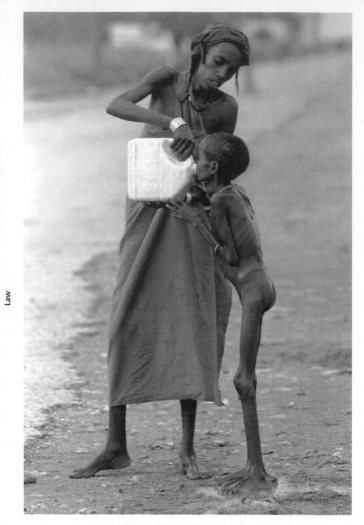

12. Severe poverty afflicts millions of people around the world.

incoherent or cast in such vague and general terms, and weakened by inevitable exclusions and exemptions, that often they appear to take away with one hand what they give with the other. In impoverished countries, modern conceptions of human rights are at times regarded with suspicion as Western or Eurocentric, failing to address the problems of starvation, poverty, and suffering that afflict many of their people. Indeed, it is asserted that they merely shore up the prevailing distribution of wealth and power.

These, and many other, doubts about the development of human rights are not to be lightly dismissed. Nor should we be under any illusion that international, or indeed domestic, declarations or the agencies that exist to implement them are adequate. They provide the contours of a strategy for improved protection. The role of the numerous NGOs, independent human rights commissions, pressure groups, and courageous individuals are of paramount importance. The growing body of law on the subject does promote a degree of optimism about the future well-being of humanity. In view of our planet's ecological despoliation and even potential nuclear immolation, it is necessary, if not essential, to conceive of rights as a weapon by which to safeguard the interests of all living things against harm, and to promote the circumstances under which they are able to flourish.

A fundamental shift in our social and economic systems and structures may be the only way in which to secure a sustainable future for our world and its inhabitants. The universal recognition of human rights seems to be a vital element in this process.

The future will undoubtedly challenge the capacity of the law not only to control domestic threats to security, but also to negotiate a rational approach to the menace of international terror. Public international law and the United Nations Charter will continue to offer the optimal touchstone by which to determine what constitutes tolerable conduct in respect of both war and peace.

'Humanitarian intervention' has in recent years become a significant feature of the international scene. There is increasing support for action to prevent or avoid the horrors of gruesome flashpoints around the world. The list seems to grow almost daily. Moreover, in a world in which the law must confront an insidious enemy within, the very foundations of international law are severely tested. This war is waged not between states, but by a clandestine international terrorist network with pernicious ambitions.

It is easy, especially for lawyers, to exaggerate the significance of the law. Yet history teaches that the law is an essential force in facilitating human progress. This is no small achievement. Without law, as Thomas Hobbes famously declared:

> there is no place for Industry, because the fruit thereof is uncertain; and consequently no Culture of the Earth, no Navigation, nor use of the commodities that may be imported by sea; no commodious Building, no instruments of moving and removing such things as require much force; no Knowledge of the face of the Earth, no account of Time, no Arts, no Letters, no Society; and which is worst of all, continual fear and danger of violent death; and the life of people, solitary, poor, nasty, brutish, and short.

If we are to survive the calamities that await us, if civilized values and justice are to prevail and endure, the law is surely indispensable.

References

Chapter 1: Law's roots

'One writer adds flesh...': Joseph Raz, 'The Rule of Law and its Virtue', *Law Quarterly Review* 93 (1977), 195.

'[B]asic institutions, concepts, and values...': Harold J. Berman, *Law and Revolution: The Formation of the Western Legal Tradition* (Harvard University Press, 1995), p. 165.

'[L]ife might be much simpler...': A. W. B. Simpson, 'The Common Law and Legal Theory', in William Twining (ed.), *Legal Theory and Common Law* (Basil Blackwell, 1986), pp. 15–16.

'[The Talmud] represents a brilliant...': H. Patrick Glenn, *On Common Laws* (Oxford University Press, 2005), p. 131.

'Islamic law...seeks constancy...': Lawrence Rosen, *The Anthropology of Justice: Law as Culture in Islamic Society* (Cambridge University Press, 1989), p. 287.

'Hindu law recognizes...': H. Patrick Glenn, *Legal Traditions of the World: Sustainable Diversity in Law*, 4th edition (Oxford University Press, 2010), p. 303.

'Like a jewel in a brooch...': H. R. Hahlo and Ellison Kahn, *The South African Legal System and Its Background* (Juta, 1968), p. 218.

'I would venture to suggest...': Albert H. Y. Chen, 'Confucian Legal Culture and its Modern Fate', in Raymond Wacks (ed.), *The New Legal Order in Hong Kong* (Hong Kong University Press, 1999), pp. 532–3.

'I often wonder...': Learned Hand, *The Spirit of Liberty: Papers and Addresses of Learned Hand*, collected, and with an introduction and notes, by Irving Dilliard (Alfred A. Knopf, 1954), p. 190.

'The law as I see it...': Alfred Denning, 'The Need for a New Equity',
  Current Legal Problems 1 (1952), 9.
'consists of two parts...': H. L. A. Hart, *The Concept of Law*, 2nd
  edition, ed. P. A. Bulloch and J. Raz (Clarendon Press, 1994), p. 156.
'Nature has placed mankind...': Jeremy Bentham, *An Introduction to
  the Principles of Morals and Legislation*, ed. J. H. Burns and H. L.
  A. Hart (Athlone Press, 1970) (*The Collected Works of Jeremy
  Bentham*, ed. J. H. Burns), chapter 1, para. 1.
'Each and every pupil told me...': Rupert Cross, *Statutory
  Interpretation* (Butterworth, 1976), preface.
Bentham on 'dog law' and 'the more antique...': quoted in Gerald J.
  Postema, *Bentham and the Common Law Tradition* (Clarendon
  Press, 1989), pp. 278–9.
'The life of the law...': Oliver Wendell Holmes, *The Common Law*
  (Dover Press, 1991), p. 1.

Chapter 2: Law's branches

'[He is] devoid of any human weakness...': A. P. Herbert, *Uncommon
  Law* (Methuen, 1969), p. 4.
'This is the Court of Chancery...': Charles Dickens, *Bleak House*,
  chapter 1.

Chapter 3: Law and morality

H. L. A. Hart, 'Positivism and the Separation of Law and Morals',
  Harvard Law Review 71 (1958), 593.
Lon L. Fuller, 'Positivism and Fidelity to Law: A Reply to Professor
  Hart', *Harvard Law Review* 71 (1958), 530.
'Unless a deliberate attempt...': *Report of the Committee on
  Homosexual Offences and Prostitution*, Chairman Sir John
  Wolfenden (Cmnd 247), para. 61.
'[T]he sole end for which...': John Stuart Mill, *On Liberty*, ed.
  Gertrude Himmelfarb (Penguin Books, 1974), pp. 72–3.
'There is disintegration...': Patrick Devlin, *The Enforcement of Morals*
  (Oxford University Press, 1965), p. 14.
'The war...': Ronald Dworkin, *Life's Dominion: An Argument about
  Abortion and Euthanasia* (HarperCollins, 1993), pp. 4 and 103.
'Killing people outside war...': Richard Dawkins, *The Selfish Gene*,
  30th anniversary edition (Oxford University Press, 2003), p. 10.

United Kingdom, Abortion Act 1967, and Section 37 of the Human
  Fertilization and Embryology Act 1990.

'[W]e should stand for a *threshold absolutism*...': Gregory Fried,
  (2014) 'Review of Uwe Steinhoff, *On the Ethics of Torture*', *Notre
  Dame Philosophical Reviews*, 2013.

'The question is not whether...': Alan Dershowitz <http://blogs.
  reuters.com/great-debate/2011/09/07/
  the-case-for-torture-warrants>.

'True law is right...': Marcus Tullius Cicero, *On the Republic/On the
  Laws*, Loeb Classical Library (Harvard University Press, 1928),
  book 3, para. 22.

Chapter 4: Courts

'courts are the capitals...': Ronald Dworkin, *Law's Empire* (Belknap
  Press, 1986), p. 407.

'[T]he public entertain...': Tom Bingham, *The Rule of Law*
  (Penguin, 2010), p. 9.

'It is an awesome thing...': Edmond N. Cahn, *The Sense of Injustice*
  (Oxford University Press, 1949), p. 133.

'A judge must decide not just...': Ronald Dworkin, *Law's Empire*
  (Belknap Press, 1986), p. 1.

H. L. A Hart, *The Concept of Law*, 3rd edition, with introduction and
  notes by L. Green, and postscript ed. J. Raz and P. A. Bulloch
  (Clarendon Press, 2012).

Ronald Dworkin, *Taking Rights Seriously* (Duckworth, 1978), p. 37.

'Trial by jury is more than an instrument of justice ': Patrick Devlin,
  Trial by Jury (Stevens & Sons, 1956), p. 41.

'[M]ediation has (on our best days)...': David A. Hoffman, 'The
  Future of ADR Practice: Three Hopes, Three Fears, and Three
  Predictions' *Negotiation Journal* 467 (2006), p. 472.

Chapter 5: Lawyers

'The lawyers have twisted it...': Charles Dickens, *Bleak House*,
  chapter 8.

'The common law folk concept...': Richard L. Abel and Philip S. C.
  Lewis, 'Lawyers in the Civil Law World', in Richard L. Abel and
  Philip S. C. Lewis (eds), *Lawyers in Society: The Civil Law World*
  (Beard Books, 2005), p. 4.

Chapter 6: The future of the law

'Existing rules and principles…': Benjamin Cardozo, *The Growth of the Law* (Yale University Press, 1921), pp. 19–20.

'We need not sacrifice our constitutional freedoms…': Philip Bobbitt, *Terror and Consent: The Wars for the Twenty-First Century* (Alfred Knopf, 2008), p. 541.

'The day may come…': Jeremy Bentham, *Introduction to the Principles of Morals and Legislation*, ed. J. H. Burns and H. L. A. Hart (Athlone Press, 1970) (*The Collected Works of Jeremy Bentham*, ed. J. H. Burns), pp. 25–6.

Lawrence Lessig, *Code: Version 2.0* (Basic Books, 2006), p. 7.

Free Software Foundation website: <http://www.fsf.org>.

'there is no place for Industry…': Thomas Hobbes, *Leviathan*, ed. M. Oakeshott (Blackwell, 1960), chapter 13.

Legal sources: A very short explanation

When referring to an article in a legal journal or a decision of a court, I have included its recognized citation. This is standard practice, and, though I have kept such references to an absolute minimum, they are there in the hope that you might wish to peruse some of these sources in their complete and original form.

The method of citing legal journals or law reviews is fairly straightforward and requires no exposition here. The subject of case citations, on the other hand, is one of huge and complex proportions that would require a chapter-length elucidation. In any event, unlike lawyers and law students of my generation (who were obliged to search the shelves of dusty tomes in pursuit of an elusive law report), today's search engines provide instant Internet access to cases merely by keying in the names of the parties. There are, in addition, an assortment of databases which provide full text retrieval of cases, legislation, and law review articles. The best known (and probably the most comprehensive) are LexisNexis and Westlaw. Both contain an extensive selection of legal documents. A number of websites, many of them free, include bailii.org, lawreports.co.uk, europa.eu, echr.coe.int, worldlii.org, and findlaw.com.

An excellent account of how to unearth the law is to be found in James A. Holland and Julian S. Webb, *Learning Legal Rules: A Student's Guide to Legal Method and Reasoning*, 8th edition (Oxford University Press, 2013), chapter 2.

In order to make sense of the references in this book, however, the following should suffice. Take the English case of *Donoghue v Stevenson* [1932] A.C. 562 (H.L.) mentioned on pages 45–6. In a civil decision such as this, the name of the case is normally dictated by those of the parties: Mrs Donoghue sued Mr Stevenson. The date in square brackets signifies that the year is an essential part of the reference. Round brackets indicate that the year is not of major importance, though it is included as a matter of course. 'A.C.' is an abbreviation of Appeal Cases, the name of the official report in which the decision appears. The number that follows is the page on which the case appears. '(H.L.)' is an abbreviation for the Judicial Committee of the House of Lords, which decided the case. That court has, as mentioned in Chapter 2, now been replaced by the Supreme Court of the United Kingdom; its judgments are cited as [2015] UKSC 88.

The approach is slightly different in the United States. For example, in the Supreme Court case of *Brown v Board of Education*, 347 U.S. 483 (1954) discussed on pages 102, 128, and 131, Brown is the plaintiff, the Board of Education the defendant. The number 347 is the volume number of the reports in which the case appears. 'U.S.' is the abbreviation of *United States Reports*. The number 483 refers to the page on which the report begins, and 1954 is the year in which the judgment was delivered.

The system adopted in Europe and several other countries, as well as a detailed account of the major common law citation conventions, and those of other courts, such as the European Court of Human Rights, are concisely set out on this fact sheet: <http://portal.solent.ac.uk/library/help/factsheets/resources/referencing-law-harvard.pdf>.

Cases discussed

Chapter 2: Law's branches

Alcock v Chief Constable of South Yorkshire Police [1992] 1 A.C. 310.
(Football stadium case discussed on pages 43–4). The quote is
from Lord Hoffmann's speech at page 314.

*Associated Provincial Picture Houses Limited v Wednesbury
Corporation* [1948] 1 K.B. 223.

Carlill v Carbolic Smoke Ball Co. [1893] 1 Q.B. 256.

Donoghue v Stevenson [1932] A.C. 562 (H.L.) at 580 per Lord Atkin.
(The 'neighbour principle' quoted on page 46.)

Hall v Brooklands Auto-Racing Club (1933) 1 K.B. 205. The 'man on
the Clapham omnibus' is first mentioned by Greer L.J.

MacPherson v Buick Motor Co. 111 N.E. 1050 (NY 1916).

Rylands v Fletcher (188) L.R. 3 H.L. 330.

New York Times v Sullivan 376 U.S. 254 (1964).

Stilk v Myrick (1809) 2 Camp. 317, 170 Eng. Rep. 1168. (The sailor
case on pages 39–40.)

Chapter 3: Law and morality

Shaw v Director of Public Prosecutions [1962] A.C. 220 (H.L.) at 267,
per Lord Reid.

Roe v Wade 410 U.S. 113 (1973).

Cruzan v Director, Missouri Department of Health 497 U.S. 261 (1990).

Airedale NHS Trust v Bland [1993] A.C. 789 at 824–5 *per* Hoffmann
L.J. and at 859 *per* Mustill L.J.

PP v HSE [2014] High Court of Ireland.

Chapter 4: Courts

Marbury v Madison (1803) 5 U.S. (1 Cranch) 137.
Brown v Board of Education of Topeka, 347 U.S. 483 (1954).

Chapter 5: Lawyers

Rondel v Worsley [1969] 1 A.C. 191 at 227 (per Lord Reid). (The
    'cab-rank' rule on pages 112–13.)
Gideon v Wainwright, 372 U.S. 335 (1963).

Chapter 6: The future of the law

Brown v Board of Education of Topeka, 347 U.S. 483 (1954).
Plessy v Ferguson, 163 U.S. 537 (1896).
Dredd Scott v Sandford, 60 U.S. 393 (1857).
Plessy v Ferguson, 163 U.S. 537 (1896).

Law

Further reading

Chapter 1: Law's roots

John N. Adams and Roger Brownsword, *Understanding Law*, 4th edition (Sweet and Maxwell, 2006).

P. S. Atiyah, *Law and Modern Society*, 2nd edition (Oxford Paperbacks, 1995).

John Austin, *The Province of Jurisprudence Determined and the Uses of the Study of Jurisprudence* (Weidenfeld and Nicolson, 1954).

J. H. Baker, *An Introduction to English Legal History*, 4th edition (LexisNexis, 2002).

Manlio Bellomo, *The Common Legal Past of Europe, 1000–1800: 4 (Studies in Medieval and Early Modern Canon Law)*, tr. Lydia G. Cochrane (Catholic University of America Press, 1995).

Jeremy Bentham, *A Fragment on Government; or, A Comment on the Commentaries*, 2nd edition (W. Pickering, 1823).

Jeremy Bentham, *An Introduction to the Principles of Morals and Legislation*, ed. J. H. Burns and H. L. A. Hart (Athlone Press, 1970) (*The Collected Works of Jeremy Bentham*, ed. J. H. Burns).

Jeremy Bentham, *Of Laws in General*, ed. H. L. A. Hart (Athlone Press, 1970) (*The Collected Works of Jeremy Bentham*, ed. J. H. Burns).

Harold J. Berman, *Law and Revolution: The Formation of the Western Legal Tradition* (Harvard University Press, 1995).

Tom Bingham, *The Rule of Law* (Penguin, 2010).

Albert H. Y. Chen, *An Introduction to the Legal System of the People's Republic of China* (Butterworths Law, Asia, 1992).

Guang Chen, Zhang Wang, Wang Chen Guang, and Zhang Xian Chu (eds), *Introduction to Chinese Law* (Sweet and Maxwell, Asia, 2001).

Richard Chisholm and Garth Nettheim, *Understanding Law: An Introduction to Australia's Legal System* (Lexis Law Publishing, 1992).

J. M. J. Chorus, *Introduction to Dutch Law*, 3rd edition (Kluwer Law International, 1998).

Andrew Clapham, *Human Rights: A Very Short Introduction* (Oxford University Press, 2007).

Council of Europe, *The Rebirth of Democracy: 12 Constitutions of Central and Eastern Europe* (Council of Europe, 1996).

François Dessemontet and Tugrul Ansay (eds), *Introduction to Swiss Law*, 3rd edition (Kluwer Law International, 2004).

Albert Venn Dicey, *Introduction to the Study of the Law of the Constitution*, ed. Roger E. Michener, 8th revised edition (Liberty Fund, 1982).

Ronald, *Taking Rights Seriously*, new impression with a reply to critics (Duckworth, 1978).

Ronald Dworkin, *Law's Empire* (Belknap Press, 1986).

Catherine Elliott, Eric Jeanpierre, and Catherine Vernon, *French Legal System*, 2nd edition (Longman, 2006).

Emily Finch and Stefan Fafinski, *Legal Skills* (Oxford University Press, 2007).

Howard D. Fisher, *The German Legal System and Legal Language*, 5th edition (Clarus Press, 2013).

George P. Fletcher and Steve Sheppard, *American Law in a Global Context: The Basics* (Oxford University Press, 2005).

Lawrence M. Friedman, *American Law in the Twentieth Century* (Yale University Press, 2002).

Lawrence M. Friedman, *American Law: An Introduction*, 2nd edition (W. W. Norton, 1999).

Lawrence M. Friedman and Rogelio Perez-Perdomo (eds), *Legal Culture in the Age of Globalization: Latin America and Latin Europe* (Stanford University Press, 2003).

Yash Ghai, *Hong Kong's New Constitutional Order: The Resumption of Chinese Sovereignty and the Basic Law*, 2nd edition (Hong Kong University Press, 1999).

Robert Gleave and Eugenia Kermeli (eds), *Islamic Law: Theory and Practice* (I.B. Tauris, 2001).

H. Patrick Glenn, *Legal Traditions of the World: Sustainable Diversity in Law* (Oxford University Press, 2007).

H. Patrick Glenn, *On Common Laws* (Oxford University Press, 2007).

H. R. Hahlo and Ellison Kahn, *The South African Legal System and Its Background* (Juta, 1968).

John Owen Haley, *The Spirit of Japanese Law* (University of Georgia Press, 2006).

Wael B. Hallaq, *An Introduction to Islamic Law* (Cambridge University Press, 2009).

Phil Harris, *Introduction to Law*, 7th edition (Cambridge University Press, 2006).

H. L. A. Hart, *The Concept of Law*, ed. P. A. Bulloch and J. Raz, 3rd edition, with an introduction by L. Green (Clarendon Press, 1994).

Thomas Hobbes, *Leviathan*, ed. M. Oakeshott (Blackwell, 1960).

Tony Honoré, *About Law: An Introduction* (Oxford University Press, 1996).

K. D. Kerameus and P. J. Kozyris, *Introduction to Greek Law*, 2nd edition (Kluwer Law International, 1988).

Michael Loewe and Edward L. Shaughnessy (eds), *The Cambridge History of Ancient China. From the Origins of Civilization to 221 BC* (Cambridge University Press, 1999).

Stanley B. Lubman, *Bird in a Cage: Legal Reform in China after Mao* (Stanford University Press, 2002).

Chibli Mallat, *Introduction to Middle Eastern Law* (Oxford University Press, 2007).

Elizabeth Martin and Jonathan Law (eds), *A Dictionary of Law*, 7th edition (Oxford University Press, 2013).

Elena Merino-Blanco, *Spanish Law and Legal System*, 2nd edition (Sweet and Maxwell, 2005).

John Henry Merryman and Rogelio Pérez-Perdomo, *The Civil Law Tradition: Introduction to the Legal Systems of Western Europe and Latin America*, 3rd edition (Stanford University Press, 2007).

S. F. C. Milsom, *Historical Foundations of the Common Law*, 2nd edition (LexisNexis, 1981).

Grant Morris, *Law Alive: The New Zealand Legal System in Context*, 3rd edition (Oxford University Press, 2014).

R. D. Mulholland, *Introduction to the New Zealand Legal System* (Butterworths Law, New Zealand, 1990).

Barry Nicholas, *An Introduction to Roman Law* (Clarendon Press, 1975).

Manfred Nowak, *Introduction to the International Human Rights Regime: No. 14* (Raoul Wallenberg Institute Series of Intergovernmental Human Rights Documentation, 2005).

Lester Bernhardt Orfield, *The Growth of Scandinavian Law* (Lawbook Exchange Ltd, 2002).

Vernon V. Palmer, *Mixed Jurisdictions Worldwide: The Third Legal Family* (Cambridge University Press, 2007).

Amanda Perreau-Saussine and James B. Murphy (eds), *The Nature of Customary Law: Legal, Historical and Philosophical Perspectives* (Cambridge University Press, 2007).

Richard A. Posner, *Law and Legal Theory in England and America* (Clarendon Press, 1996).

Gerald J. Postema, *Bentham and the Common Law Tradition* (Clarendon Press, 1989).

Ravi Prakesh, *The Constitution, Fundamental Rights and Judicial Activism in India* (Mangal Deep, India, 1998).

John Rawls, *A Theory of Justice* (Oxford University Press, 1973).

John Rawls, *Political Liberalism* (Columbia University Press, 1993).

Geoffrey Robertson, *Crimes Against Humanity: The Struggle for Global Justice* (Penguin Books, 2006).

Lawrence Rosen, *The Anthropology of Justice: Law as Culture in Islamic Society* (Cambridge University Press, 1989).

William A. Schabas, *An Introduction to the International Criminal Court*, 2nd edition (Cambridge University Press, 2004).

Brij Kishore Sharma, *Introduction to the Constitution of India* (Prentice-Hall, India, 2005).

Robert J. Sharpe and Kent Roach, *The Charter of Rights and Freedoms*, 3rd edition (Essentials of Canadian Law, Irwin Law, 2005).

Mathias Siems, *Comparative Law* (Cambridge University Press, 2014).

A. W. B. Simpson, *Invitation to Law* (Blackwell, 1988).

Gary Slapper, *How the Law Works* (Collins, 2007).

Gary Slapper and David Kelly, *The English Legal System: 2014–2015*, 15th edition (Routledge, 2014).

Peter Stein, *Roman Law in European History* (Cambridge University Press, 1999).

Alexander Vereshchagin, *Judicial Law-Making in Post-Soviet Russia* (UCL Press, 2007).

Raymond Wacks (ed.), *The Future of the Law in Hong Kong* (Oxford University Press, China, 1991).

Raymond Wacks (ed.), *The New Legal Order in Hong Kong* (Hong Kong University Press, 1999).

Raymond Wacks, *Philosophy of Law: A Very Short Introduction*, 2nd edition (Oxford University Press, 2014).

Raymond Wacks, *Understanding Jurisprudence: An Introduction to Legal Theory*, 4th edition (Oxford University Press, 2015).

Ian Ward, *A Critical Introduction to European Law*, 3rd edition (Cambridge University Press, 2009).

Thomas Wegerich and Anke Freckmann, *The German Legal System* (Sweet and Maxwell, 1999).

Peter Wesley-Smith, *An Introduction to the Hong Kong Legal System*, 3rd edition (Oxford University Press, China, 1999).

Glanville Williams and A. T. H. Smith, *Learning the Law*, 15th edition (Sweet and Maxwell, 2013).

Konrad Zweigert and Hein Kötz, *An Introduction to Comparative Law*, tr. Tony Weir (Clarendon Press, 1998).

Chapter 2: Law's branches

Paul Craig and Gráinne de Búrca, *EU Law: Text, Cases, and Materials*, 5th edition (Oxford University Press, 2011).

Helen Fenwick and Gavin Phillipson, *Text, Cases and Materials: Public Law and Human Rights*, 3rd edition (Routledge Cavendish, 2010).

George P. Fletcher and Steve Sheppard, *American Law in a Global Context: The Basics* (Oxford University Press, 2005).

D. J. Harris, M. O'Boyle, E. R. Bates, and C. M. Buckley, *Law of the European Convention on Human Rights*, 3rd edition (Oxford University Press, 2014).

James A. Holland and Julian S. Webb, *Learning Legal Rules: A Student's Guide to Legal Method and Reasoning*, 8th edition (Oxford University Press, 2013).

Ian Loveland, *Constitutional Law, Administrative Law, and Human Rights: A Critical Introduction*, 6th edition (Oxford University Press, 2012).

Alastair Mowbray, *Cases and Materials on the European Convention on Human Rights*, 3rd edition (Oxford University Press, 2012).

Bernadette Rainey, Elizabeth Wicks, and Clare Ovey, *Jacobs, White & Ovey: The European Convention on Human Rights*, 6th edition (Oxford University Press, 2014).

Chapter 3: Law and morality

Thomas Aquinas, *Summa Theologiae*, in *Selected Political Writings*, tr. J. G. Dawson, ed. P. D'Entrèves (Blackwell, 1970; reprint of 1959 edition).

Aristotle, *Nichomachean Ethics*, tr. H. Rackham (Loeb Classical Library, Heineman, 1938).

Ronald Dworkin, *Life's Dominion: An Argument about Abortion and Euthanasia* (HarperCollins, 1993).

John Finnis, *Natural Law and Natural Rights* (Clarendon Press, 1980).

John Finnis, *Fundamentals of Ethics* (Georgetown University Press, 1983).

John Finnis (ed.), *Natural Law* (Dartmouth, 1991).

Lon Luvois Fuller, *The Morality of Law*, revised edition (Yale University Press, 1969).

Robert P. George, *In Defense of Natural Law* (Oxford University Press, 1999).

Joseph Raz, *The Authority of Law: Essays on Law and Morality* (Clarendon Press, 1979).

Joseph Raz, *The Morality of Freedom* (Oxford University Press, 1986).

Joseph Raz, *Ethics in the Public Domain: Essays in the Morality of Law and Politics* (Clarendon Press, 1994).

Chapter 4: Courts

Aharon Barak, *The Judge in a Democracy* (Princeton University Press, 2006).

Marcel Berlins and Clare Dyer, *The Law Machine*, 5th edition (Penguin Books, 2000).

Alan Dershowitz, *Is There a Right to Remain Silent?: Coercive Interrogation and the Fifth Amendment After 9/11* (Oxford University Press, 2008).

Ronald Dworkin, *Justice in Robes* (Belknap Press, 2006).

Jeffrey Goldsworthy (ed.), *Interpreting Constitutions: A Comparative Study* (Oxford University Press, 2007).

J. A. G. Griffith, *The Politics of the Judiciary*, 5th edition (Fontana Press, 1997).

Carlo Guarnieri, Patrizia Pederzoli, and Cheryl Thomas, *The Power of Judges: A Comparative Study of Courts and Democracy* (Oxford University Press, 2002).

Sally J. Kenney, *Gender and Justice: Why Women in the Judiciary Really Matter* (Routledge, 2012).

John Morison, Kieran McEvoy, and Gordon Anthony (eds), *Judges, Transition, and Human Rights* (Oxford University Press, 2007).

David Pannick, *Judges* (Oxford University Press, 1987).

David Pannick, *I Have to Move My Car: Tales of Unpersuasive Advocates and Injudicious Judges* (Hart, 2008).

Alan Paterson, *Final Judgment: The Last Law Lords and the Supreme Court* (Hart, 2013).

William H. Rehnquist, *The Supreme Court* (Vintage Books USA, 2002).

Shimon Shetreet and Sophie Turenne, *Judges on Trial: The Independence and Accountability of the English Judiciary*, 2nd edition (Cambridge University Press, 2013).

Robert Stevens, *The English Judges: Their Role in the Changing Constitution* (Hart Publishing, 2005).

Chapter 5: Lawyers

Richard L. Abel, *American Lawyers* (Oxford University Press, 1991).

Richard L. Abel and Philip S. C. Lewis (eds), *Lawyers in Society: The Common Law World* (University of California Press, 1988).

Richard L. Abel and Philip S. C. Lewis, 'Lawyers in the Civil Law World', in Richard L. Abel and Philip S. C. Lewis (eds), *Lawyers in Society: The Civil Law World* (Beard Books, 2005).

Alan Dershowitz, *The Best Defense* (Vintage Books, 1983).

Mary Jane Mossman, *The First Women Lawyers: A Comparative Study of Gender, Law and the Legal Professions* (Hart Publishing, 2006).

David Pannick, *Advocates* (Oxford University Press, 1992).

Wilfrid R. Prest, *The Rise of the Barristers: A Social History of the English Bar, 1590–1640* (Clarendon Press, 1991).

Richard Susskind, *Tomorrow's Lawyers* (Oxford University Press, 2013).

Chapter 6: The future of the law

David Bainbridge, *Introduction to Computer Law*, 6th edition (Longman, 2007).

Colin J. Bennett, *Regulating Privacy: Data Protection and Public Policy in Europe and the United States* (Cornell University Press, 1992).

Philip Bobbitt, *Terror and Consent: The Wars for the Twenty-First Century* (Alfred Knopf, 2008).

James Boyle, *Shamans, Software and Spleens: Law and the Construction of the Information Society* (Harvard University Press, 1997).

Roger Brownsword and Morag Goodwin, *Law and the Technologies of the Twenty-First Century* (Cambridge University Press, 2012).

David DeGrazia, *Animal Rights: A Very Short Introduction* (Oxford University Press, 2002).

Lilian Edwards and Charlotte Waelde (eds), *Law and the Internet: A Framework for Electronic Commerce*, 2nd edition (Hart Publishing, 2004).

Andrew T. Kenyon and Megan Richardson (eds), *New Dimensions in Privacy Law: International and Comparative Perspectives* (Cambridge University Press, 2006).

Graeme Laurie, *Genetic Privacy: A Challenge to Medico-Legal Norms* (Cambridge University Press, 2002).

Lawrence Lessig, *Code: Version 2.0* (Basic Books, 2006).

Ian Lloyd, *Information Technology Law*, 7th edition (Oxford University Press, 2014).

Andrew Murray, *Information Technology Law: The Law and Society*, 2nd edition (Oxford University Press, 2013).

Chris Reed, *Making Laws for Cyberspace* (Oxford University Press, 2012).

Tom Regan, *The Case for Animal Rights* (University of California Press, 2004).

Jeffrey Rosen, *The Unwanted Gaze: The Destruction of Privacy in America* (Vintage Books, 2001).

Peter Singer (ed.), *In Defense of Animals: The Second Wave*, 2nd edition (Blackwell, 2005).

Daniel J. Solove, *The Digital Person: Technology and Privacy in the Information Age* (New York University Press, 2006).

Raymond Wacks, *Personal Information: Privacy and the Law* (Clarendon Press, 1989).

Raymond Wacks (ed.), *Privacy* (Dartmouth, 1993).

Raymond Wacks, *Privacy and Media Freedom* (Oxford University Press, 2013).

Raymond Wacks, *Privacy: A Very Short Introduction*, 2nd edition (Oxford University Press, 2015).

Index

CITIZENSHIP
A Very Short Introduction
Richard Bellamy

Interest in citizenship has never been higher. But what does it mean to be a citizen of a modern, complex community? Why is citizenship important? Can we create citizenship, and can we test for it? In this fascinating Very Short Introduction, Richard Bellamy explores the answers to these questions and more in a clear and accessible way. He approaches the subject from a political perspective, to address the complexities behind the major topical issues. Discussing the main models of citizenship, exploring how ideas of citizenship have changed through time from ancient Greece to the present, and examining notions of rights and democracy, he reveals the irreducibly political nature of citizenship today.

'Citizenship is a vast subject for a short introduction, but Richard Bellamy has risen to the challenge with aplomb.'

Mark Garnett, TLS

www.oup.com/vsi

Economics
A Very Short Introduction
Partha Dasgupta

Economics has the capacity to offer us deep insights into some of the most formidable problems of life, and offer solutions to them too. Combining a global approach with examples from everyday life, Partha Dasgupta describes the lives of two children who live very different lives in different parts of the world: in the Mid-West USA and in Ethiopia. He compares the obstacles facing them, and the processes that shape their lives, their families, and their futures. He shows how economics uncovers these processes, finds explanations for them, and how it forms policies and solutions.

> 'An excellent introduction . . . presents mathematical and statistical findings in straightforward prose.'
>
> Financial Times

www.oup.com/vsi

THE EUROPEAN UNION

A Very Short Introduction

John Pinder & Simon Usherwood

This *Very Short Introduction* explains the European Union in plain English. Fully updated for 2007 to include controversial and current topics such as the Euro currency, the EU's enlargement, and its role in ongoing world affairs, this accessible guide shows how and why the EU has developed from 1950 to the present. Covering a range of topics from the Union's early history and the ongoing interplay between 'eurosceptics' and federalists, to the single market, agriculture, and the environment, the authors examine the successes and failures of the EU, and explain the choices that lie ahead in the 21st century.

FREE SPEECH
A Very Short Introduction
Nigel Warburton

'I disapprove of what you say, but I will defend to the death your right to say it' This slogan, attributed to Voltaire, is frequently quoted by defenders of free speech. Yet it is rare to find anyone prepared to defend all expression in every circumstance, especially if the views expressed incite violence. So where do the limits lie? What is the real value of free speech? Here, Nigel Warburton offers a concise guide to important questions facing modern society about the value and limits of free speech: Where should a civilized society draw the line? Should we be free to offend other people's religion? Are there good grounds for censoring pornography? Has the Internet changed everything? This Very Short Introduction is a thought-provoking, accessible, and up-to-date examination of the liberal assumption that free speech is worth preserving at any cost.

'The genius of Nigel Warburton's *Free Speech* lies not only in its extraordinary clarity and incisiveness. Just as important is the way Warburton addresses freedom of speech - and attempts to stifle it - as an issue for the 21st century. More than ever, we need this book.'

Denis Dutton, University of Canterbury, New Zealand

www.oup.com/vsi

HUMAN RIGHTS
A Very Short Introduction
Andrew Clapham

An appeal to human rights in the face of injustice can be a heartfelt and morally justified demand for some, while for others it remains merely an empty slogan. Taking an international perspective and focusing on highly topical issues such as torture, arbitrary detention, privacy, health and discrimination, this *Very Short Introduction* will help readers to understand for themselves the controversies and complexities behind this vitally relevant issue. Looking at the philosophical justification for rights, the historical origins of human rights and how they are formed in law, Andrew Clapham explains what our human rights actually are, what they might be, and where the human rights movement is heading.

www.oup.com/vsi

INTERNATIONAL RELATIONS
A Very Short Introduction
Paul Wilkinson

Of undoubtable relevance today, in a post-9-11 world of growing political tension and unease, this *Very Short Introduction* covers the topics essential to an understanding of modern international relations. Paul Wilkinson explains the theories and the practice that underlies the subject, and investigates issues ranging from foreign policy, arms control, and terrorism, to the environment and world poverty. He examines the role of organizations such as the United Nations and the European Union, as well as the influence of ethnic and religious movements and terrorist groups which also play a role in shaping the way states and governments interact. This up-to-date book is required reading for those seeking a new perspective to help untangle and decipher international events.

www.oup.com/vsi

Neoliberalism
A Very Short Introduction
Manfred B. Steger & Ravi K. Roy

Anchored in the principles of the free-market economics, 'neoliberalism' has been associated with such different political leaders as Ronald Reagan, Margaret Thatcher, Bill Clinton, Tony Blair, Augusto Pinochet, and Junichiro Koizumi.So is neoliberalism doomed or will it regain its former glory? Will reform-minded G-20 leaders embark on a genuine new course or try to claw their way back to the neoliberal glory days of the Roaring Nineties? Is there a viable alternative to neoliberalism? Exploring the origins, core claims, and considerable variations of neoliberalism, this Very Short Introduction offers a concise and accessible introduction to one of the most debated 'isms' of our time.

'This book is a timely and relevant contribution to this urgent contemporary topic.'

I. K. Gujral, Former Prime Minister of India

www.oup.com/vsi

SOCIAL MEDIA
Very Short Introduction

Join our community
www.oup.com/vsi

- Join us online at the official Very Short Introductions **Facebook** page.
- Access the thoughts and musings of our authors with our online **blog**.
- Sign up for our monthly **e-newsletter** to receive information on all new titles publishing that month.
- Browse the full range of Very Short Introductions online.
- Read **extracts** from the Introductions for free.
- Visit our library of **Reading Guides**. These guides, written by our expert authors will help you to question again, why you think what you think.
- If you are a teacher or lecturer you can order inspection copies quickly and simply via our website.